Collegiality

AND OTHER BALLADS

feminist poems by
male and non-binary allies

Collegiality

AND OTHER BALLADS

feminist poems by
male and non-binary allies

INTRODUCED & EDITED BY
SHAMAYITA SEN

Hawakal
PUBLISHERS
New Delhi | Calcutta

HAWAKAL
New Delhi | Calcutta

HAWAKAL PUBLISHERS
70 B/9 Amritpuri, East of Kailash, New Delhi 65
33/1/2 K B Sarani, Mall Road, Calcutta 80

info@hawakal.com
www.hawakal.com

Cover designed by Bitan Chakraborty

First edition (paperback) May 2021

ISBN: 978-81-950350-6-9

Price: INR 450 | USD 14.99

For

Dida, Maa

and

the revolutions that are yet to come

She stripped herself bare
and scrawled with charcoal
all over her body: 'non-negotiable.'

Then she poured petrol
from head to foot
and set herself afire.

K. SATCHIDANANDAN
"Non-negotiable"

there was little feminist education for critical consciousness
teaching us how to respect our bodies in an anti-sexist way

bell hooks, *Feminism is for Everybody: Passionate Politics*

UNEQUAL MUSIC

Feminism is the name of a unique battle. I write this with a momentous verdict just behind me. Derek Chauvin, a former Minneapolis police officer, has been convicted of murder and manslaughter almost a year after the May evening when he held his knee down on the neck of the handcuffed George Floyd for nine minutes and twenty-nine seconds till Floyd's heart gave away. Floyd was black, Chauvin white. The latter was suspected of passing a counterfeit currency note; you do the rest of the math. How does one human being do this to another?

In the last nine and a half minutes of his life, Floyd experienced violence whose many languages have not been a secret to women across India and throughout the world. George Floyd died on the streets of Minneapolis, at the intersection of 38th Street and Chicago Avenue, since then a hallowed spot of protest and remembrance. That too scripts a different trajectory of violence—and consequently, an arc of resistance that intersects as well as departs from racial oppression.

Violence against women, unforgettably metaphorized here in the poem by K. Satchidanandan, for a great part, happens inside what people consider their safest space in the world. *The home*. This is where the struggle of a woman, or someone minoritized by their sexual identity, becomes a unique one among the daily battles raged worldwide by people of oppressed racial, class, or caste backgrounds, even when different excluded identities merge to create many layers of unbelonging. The great part of the fight for the liberation of race, class, and caste happens in the public sphere, though they bleed into the private sphere incessantly. But for the vast majority of people in the world, a close and intimate relationship with someone from a different race, caste, and even class, primarily remains a matter of choice.

Rooted in the politics of intimacy, this feminist project is unique. No human individual inhabits a world where they have not been, at least for a period, been in an intimate relationship with someone from different sex. Sleeping with the adversary never had a more primitive meaning—or sleeping inside the enemy, or sleeping with the enemy inside you—howsoever you want to name the male child inside the mother, or the mother with the male child inside her. Feminists as wide-ranging as Rokeya Sakhawat Hossain in "Sultana's Dream" and Valerie Solanas in the *SCUM Manifesto* (Society for Cutting out Men) have variously imagined worlds free of men or male agency, and often for very good reason, but such acts of sexual cleansing have remained in the realm of the fictitious.

That is why the feminist and non-binary struggle remains one fought significantly, perhaps overwhelmingly, in the private sphere. Both history and reality around us tell us that it is also a crucial public battle, not merely for things like an equitable opportunity in the workplace or access to civil and democratic rights, but against the very public, historically entrenched order of patriarchy, which like an invisible and inevitable force, engulfs all sexes and genders. That's what Virginia Woolf called for in *Three Guineas*, to remake a hyper-masculine, heavily militarized public sphere in the image of the private sphere to which women had been historically restricted—to educate the former with the humbly earned virtues of the latter. Woolf's vision of the world is androgynous, just as she imagined her character Orlando to be—Lord Orlando becomes Lady Orlando after a couple of hundred years of "his" life, to transform into the tall, boyish, sharp-featured, female author in wartime England that its actual creator would become herself.

Woolf's androgyny also contained her bisexuality, or more appropriately, her queerness, the dissident desire that undoes traditional binaries between dominant forms of gender and sexual desire. We contain multitudes within us, scarcely a few among which can be accommodated by our lifestyle choices and social representation of ourselves. Society would not be society if it were not norm-driven. What choice do we have but to live forever at a slight angle to socially crafted norms? What choice do men have but to become allies to the female and non-binary struggle against patriarchy that imprisons all sexes and sexualities—what choice but to plead for perpetual forgiveness for the havoc creaked by insidious as well as toxic masculinity? An overwhelming number of men don't ally themselves to this struggle, doubtless deluded by the illusion of advantage patriarchy offers them. But this delusion keeps them poor and stunted, a long way from the realization of their true potential and of the real worth of the human universe. McDuff, too, was woman-born—he was "but snatched from the womb early"—as we all are, early, late, or on time, entwined in a mutual company that is inextricably intimate, sweaty and prickly, pleasurable and unimaginably hurtful. What choice do we have but to worry about the lines that separate our gender and our desire into binary oppositions convenient for a society that remains patriarchal and heteronormative in the service of forces that are more powerful than human beings?

No wonder male poets here speak in voices that long to be feminine or bemoan the failure to be so. In Amit Shankar Saha's poem, it becomes the necessary dream of 'The Outsider' even as the voice carries a cry of futility: "I cannot write a feminist poem / for my mother is dead." Death on the other end, of a child in her womb, drapes the dark around Boudhayan Mukherjee's poetic voice in "Elegy." Fluid gender is a rich crown of thorns for Chand, speaking starkly: "My gender fucks with your mind and categories / And wants to fuck you." But a man's body is always that of a woman's too; its intimate debt is not just to a mother, but to others like her, aunts and grandmothers who give birth to kin many times over, who nourish us through our lives, and far beyond their own. In Sumallya Mukhopadhyay's poems, myths in the family stretch, expand into infinity, become planetary, while Manik Sharma's poetic voice imagines the voices of their grandpa and grandma: "They were angry at each other for getting old, and / for having crumpled skin that read like trashed paper." But a quotidian refrain, no less powerful: "I hardly ever saw my mother. I was with you." drive the music in Souradeep Roy's poem about the nourishing specter of a grandmother, claiming kinship with Subhrasankar Das's unforgettable, "Zero," where a beloved aunt catches fish as if they were fingers that had slipped away. The lyric of the woman as dwelling in continuity with nature, a powerful running strain in this collection, also recalls the poetry of Kinshuk Gupta, where flora and fauna, snakes and plant-tendril, the animate and the inanimate entangle to haunting beauty, and the words of Amlanjyoti Goswami, which paint the image of the newlywed girl about to leave the home she remembers as "mud banks, sunlit alleys," and "silver flying fishes." Houses bare their souls, especially when people leave or new people arrive to join their fold. "The old house blushed / Twilight hues painting a shy smile" in Raja Chakraborty's poem, "Of Houses" when the newlywed wife crosses the threshold to call the house her own.

But visceral intimacy is not limited to mothers, aunts, and grandmothers. There is another woman who clears the debris of everyday life, soaks its dirt and grime, whose brutal reality is deified time and again in these poems. It is the invisible omnipresence of the other divinity, the woman as a domestic laborer, the household help, whether kindred or hired. The powerful futility of her cry is recorded in Abhay K's "A Maid's Monologue," as well as in the gnarled kitchen of the old woman in Aditya Shankar's moving poem of "wrinkled hands" and "dirt" that "takes over the rims of her casseroles and tumblers." The raging lyricism of the excerpts from Khal Torabully's "Voices from the Aapravasi Ghat" crystallizes the historical violence done to the coolie woman as well as her brutal question: "How can an object of Desire be a subject of Empire? / How Sahib?" The construction worker who piles bricks atop her head in Goirick Brahmachari's "As I Watch the Road" lights, at the end of a tiring day, her bidi, in a gesture where disdain and despair melt into each other interminably. Ankush Banerjee tells a mythical story of labor and abuse—of the woman whose limp body was dragged out of a pond one day, who, resuscitated, was named Kalindi, to become a maid to the family. But she also becomes a myth that dwarfs the real, as Yajnaseni in Dibyajyoti Sarma's powerful lines: "What would you do, Yajnaseni? / Cook your flesh? Cook the flesh of your daughters?"

Sexual labor remains unmentionable that continues to bind certain women to public or domestic forms of exploitation, whether for marriage or commerce. Basab Mondal creates a poem about "the moll carrying the unborn / in the dark of her womb," where the haunting shadow of a streetwalking woman attains a mythical unreality. In "The Silent Lane," Milan Mondal etches the evening of a prostitute who is ready to accept any patron, "for bargaining is useless." The shadow of a streetwalker in narrow, dusky alleys is an image that draws me like a magnet, especially the life of a prostitute as a performer. The darkness associated with the life of an actress as seen through the eyes of her young son shaped one of my own novels, one especially dear to me for reasons hard to explain. Here too, domesticity is no safe refuge for a woman from sexual oppression. This comes viscerally alive in Paresh Tiwari's poem, "Surviving Marital Rape," where the most significant option for the victim is to say "'No.' Loud enough for the walls to come crashing down." As predatorial greed makes the doe's flesh her greatest enemy, the world of male lust renders a woman's body her enemy, a vicious paradox heart-rendingly captured in Durga Prasad Panda's poem, "Her Body."

Society's admission of violence against women continues to be riddled with ironies. Allan Kolski Horwitz's poem "Census" narrates a dystopian accounting of battered women, where "standing in front of the enumerators / it was almost like being famous / this being counted as if you count." But in Ammar Aziz's poetic voice, there is no anodyne of anonymity, as it is the father who beats the mother, as that's the norm in that town, "Where women / Often became nightingales / Disappearing into the stars." Sexual onslaught takes on a vitriolic form when bolstered by caste privilege. Chandramohan Sathyanathan gives pointed shape to caste-driven oppression of sexual freedom in his poem "On Inter-caste Love" and paints a flaming picture of the Dalit woman poet: "Her book of poems / is a treatise on disheveled hair / and tresses on fire." Madhu Raghavendra outlines, in the cryptic language of commerce, the hypocrisies of sex and caste that shape matrimonial ads. The nurturing sexual power of women throbs to violent life in another poem he writes, where women withhold sex to end war: "I am a woman; I can freeze civil wars / between my thighs / let your arousal increase / peace. / Once we win over your gory arms / let's make love in peace." Maaz Bin Bilal, too, travels to parts of the world where the oppression and the liberation of women are conditioned by yet another inexorable determinant, religion: "Yeah, you're right, I drove that Audi, / in prison, I am, I am the woman of Saudi!"

When a man takes an honest and searing look at a woman and her journey, the female form appears no less mythical than real. Alan Britt's "Myth of the Baker's Daughter" is an Ovidian work where "They say the owl / used to be a baker's daughter / with wild hyacinth hair." Metamorphosis becomes an intricate, artistic process in Alvin Pang's poetry; between plant, women, and sculpture, a different awakening arrives in Amal Joseph Mathew's lines, where "The painter recalls the face of God; it is a woman." Bibhu Padhi writes a poem like a silhouette, "All through the long night," where light and shadow recreate the entropy of human life. Debarshi Mitra's "Genesis" articulates an origin story that also feels like an apocalypse, where the endless expanse of one's memory is a sea that mysteriously contains the unborn. Ra Sh writes witty poems of the quick and disastrous myth of our sexual identities where at the end of the catastrophe, "Emasculated Androgen and / stitched up Estrogen have fled. / They are said to be living / in an island named / Dopamine." The abstract gets slithering body in Riccardo Duranti's minute carvings of poems while "She felt her mind curling up / around the wind / and a kite was born out of her will." Dustin Pickering's sharp, corrosive poems trade words for bullets, shatter male diplomacy to evoke the ritual potential of women warriors. The true reservoir in Gopal Lahiri's poem "Dark Reservoir" is the human mind, swirled to turbulence by feelings, images, and memory. Folklore might claim lizards as bringing good luck, but in Inam Hussain Begg Mullick's poem of tender reality, "Fear of lizards," revulsion for rats, lizards, and cockroaches shapes identifiable memorable forms. The ploy to place the mind above the body was a masculine one, and Soumik Kumar De, in "An Ode to Skin," lays bare the power of naked skin, its infinite capacity for pleasure and suffering.

Human relationships, in these poems, holds the

weight of futurity and the ethereal breath of pastness. Old women, young girls, strangers with vacant stares who claim kinship by sharing the earth with you, perhaps anonymous physical proximity. The old woman in "Bed No 187," in Sankhet Mhatre's poem asks, "*If I die here, will you take me back to my village?*" The time comes when "She smiled and wrapped her wrinkles around me / like that is the only gift she could give / before going to sleep." Youth, too, holds the deep power of promise. "The Girl of Fifteen," in the poem named after her by Sarabjeet Garcha, "dares / the tarmac vapours rising up / to become her noonday bandanna," making fierce generosity the very core of her being: "She writes the one rule / only a woman knows by birth: / *In my house, nobody dies of hunger*." For Vivekanand Selvaraj, Bharat Mata, in the poem named after her, was an unassuming, unremarkable classmate, who had "Braces and the accompanying / smile, hanging off her sword like a traitor's gut, / Saree draped like white waves with / tri-color foam and a fiery ball on her usually / bare forehead...", deceptive in her un-remarkableness, baring her vulnerability before physical punishment in the most bruising way. Human qualities, in the meantime, get gendered traits. If "coercion" is imagined as a "many trait," it forces Tim Kahl to ask: "So when / I say, leave me to my knitting—does this make / me a feminist?"

As men are born of mothers, sometimes they father daughters. Watching a daughter grow is a musical, unconscious lesson in feminism for fathers who wish to learn. In scripting the lyric of possible and fictional learning for a daughter, Umar Nizarudeen etches a whole universe of meaning—of what the word "consummation" can mean for the growing girl, after she has stumbled upon it in a dictionary. In Kiriti Sengupta's witty, deeply revealing poem "The Y-Gene," we get another script—that of a possible relationship between girls and education. The irony of wishing a daughter to call her "Srividya" comes full circle when a male child arrives instead, growing up into a boy who, returning from school one day, identifies, to his mother, girls as the classmates who "sit on the left side." But alas, patriarchy ensures that male mentoring of young women reincarnate as new acts of abuse and oppression. Lawrence Schimel's poem indeed offers a chilling fairy tale for writers, especially female writers who fall prey to male mentorship. The female writing student gives up her own writing voice, her very identity, at the behest of her male writing teacher, seeking his love and becoming his mistress in the process, only to discover that his wife was once a writer too, who gave up her own writing merely to be content to be the wife of a philandering, successful writer.

Mentorship and poetry and the tangled reality of the female artist give me the most unsettling pause. I was honored and hesitant in equal parts when the editor and the publisher asked me to write a foreword to this collection; the hesitation came no less from my own maleness than from my identity as a novelist asked to speak on poetry. But I floated along with the breeze of a conviction then not shared with anyone beyond a few friends, that which was rooted in the anticipated worlding of a new novel where I seek to tell the story of a female poet in a college caught in the intimate throes of mentorship, sucking her energy as much from an erotic Plato in *The Symposium* as from Drona's cruelty to Ekalavya. What are the ethical limits of mentorship? Of the obligations of poetry? Having read this collection, I take stronger heart—that men can write about women, write as women, no less than they can create poetry and music about the horrors men have created for women, horrors which they must own up, and the horrors created by the concrete abstraction called patriarchy that goes beyond individuals of any sex, but which always corrupts the scale to let men win in the end, just as a Brahmin guru was not above doing for his princely student, at the cost of a low-caste aspirant. I cannot think of more intricate, beautiful poetry of pain and guilt as this collection. Do read these poems and be stunned by the painful aesthetic violence and inequity can create in the strangest of ways.

SAIKAT MAJUMDAR
May 2021
New Delhi

Saikat Majumdar, professor of English & Creative Writing at Ashoka University, is the author of three novels, most recently, *The Scent of God*. He has also published a book of criticism, *Prose of the World* (2013), a work of nonfiction, *College* (2018), and a co-edited collection of essays, *The Critic as Amateur* (2019). His new novel, *The Middle Finger*, a college campus novel about poetry and mentorship, will be published in fall 2021.

MEN, INCLUSION, AND FEMINISM

Much has been written and said about feminist politics, making us believe that the world is changing slowly and steadily. But for most parts, the world has changed in verse, not in action. I remember the first conscious feminist words that were uttered to me in middle school. Our Physics teacher, in a passing comment, pointed out to us how most Mathematics problem sums presuppose a 'he' in charge of buying goods, indicating not only that language is essentially gendered but also that we entrust men with buying, selling, and decision-making powers. I believe much has happened since. In India and abroad, women in rural and urban spaces have been offered tools that have 'empowered' them to recognize patriarchal violence at home and work. We are aware that gender is a social construct and a performance[1]. However, women empowerment has not quite served the purpose; it has not eradicated gender violence.

Women empowerment puts the onus of social uplift upon women. It weaponizes female experiences, women's struggles, and the emotional labor of survivors. To quantify social evolution, this anthology, very much in tune with the fourth wave of feminism, puts the onus onto those who are historically and structurally in socially privileged positions of power: men, white or upper caste. This collection aims at inducting contemporary male poets into active feminist politics. We believe no equilibrium can be attempted in a society without the ones in systemic power willing to speak up in solidarity with those suppressed since times immemorial. Of course, male poets will write without the lived experiences of female suffering, but most political writing *is* invoked from worries locked up in the human subconscious.

The idea behind this anthology must have slowly germinated in me since the time I realized I had had a gender-neutral upbringing, or during the many cooking sessions with *Baba* as we both waited for *Maa* to return home from her election duty, or when my parents enrolled me in Bharatnatyam[2] as well as martial art classes so that their child may grow up into a well-rounded person, and so that my gender may not determine my vocational interest. I understood gender is fluid after moving to Delhi through interactions and exchanges with a vibrant group of people at university. I shall be ever grateful to my professors, friends, and colleagues who helped me open my mind to this world beyond its confines of gender binary. Feminism, for me, is this ability to find oneself in the world, in any form one chooses to—to own one's body and to be able to see beyond gender as a notion constricting human lives.

When I began thinking of this anthology's theme and structure, I was concerned if the time is apt for a work such as this. That is, at a time when women have finally owned up to their narratives, are telling their stories, and forming solidarity, is it essential we enquire after male poets' perspectives on feminism? The Me Too movement (2017)[3] exposed sexual violators at educational institutes and workplaces. This watershed moment served as an eye-opener for society. For the first time, perpetrators (and not survivors) were held responsible for a sexual offense. The movement shifted the lens of scrutiny from female bodies to male intention and directed us to think through nuances of sexual misconduct.

Two of my favorite poems from the collection are K. Satchidanandan's "Non-negotiable" and Paresh Tiwari's "Surviving Marital Rape" because of the sheer emotion they evoked on my first read. Both speak of the pangs of victimhood. The reader is rendered hopeless, wondering whether survivors ever get over traumatic life experiences. Patriarchal violence remains at the core of other poems. Kinshuk Gupta's "How Our Sisters Live and Die" is written in memory of Dr. Priyanka Reddy. Allan Kolski Horwitz's "Census" is a tale of resilience that characterizes survivors' instincts. Khal Torabully, through his use of heteroglossia[4], shares excerpts from the narrative of a female coolie who is reduced to a mere 'police case' post suffering brutalization during her journey across 'dark waters.'

In contrast, Madhu Raghavendra's "Conflict" advocates non-violent resistance through its reference to 'sex strike,' a practice to bring back peace in specific communities—'I am a woman; I can freeze civil wars between my thighs....' Chandramohan Sathyanathan writes keenly on questions of beauty and desirability. In his poems, "Plus Sized Poem" and "Portrait of a Poet as a Young Woman," he establishes beauty as an elite, capitalist construct. Kiriti Sengupta points out gender stereotypes prevalent in Indian society. In "The Y-Gene," he writes, 'After school he (son) tells his mother, *Girls sit on the left side*.' Gender stereotypes normalize the belief that girls (and women) deserve little to no care and compassion. Sengupta directs us towards what bell hooks says—'there was little feminist education' to develop 'critical consciousness' and revere ourselves and 'our bodies in an anti-sexist way.'[5]

As I continued to work on the anthology, multiple questions dangled before me. I wondered whether one must be a feminist to compose feminist poetry? But isn't Feminism an ever-evolving ideology? Can anyone ever be an 'ideal feminist?' Again, isn't it heterogeneity that gives life to an anthology! The least I did while choosing work was not to include poems that offer voyeuristic pleasure. I was wont to question: What pertains to feminist writing by men? Should it only be about feminist issues such as consent, patriarchal violence, social bindings of heterosexual relationships, etcetera? Or, should it focus on men writing about themselves sans machismo, sans violent metaphors, sans the male gaze?

Of course, social evils such as female foeticide, female infanticide, mutilation of female genitalia, and corrective rape, which are still prevalent in certain cultures, require legal and governmental interferences to bring about changes in the patriarchal mindset. But, it is time to ask other pertinent questions: In apparently progressive urban elite spaces where intimate violence such as domestic violence and sexual offence is on the rise, how is one to develop a feminist conscience or the tools of feminist parenting? I believe we have moved beyond the initial phase of acknowledging problems that mar patriarchal society. Now, we should look for active solutions to be able to live well in heteronormative[6] familial spaces. Feminist politics, unfortunately, fails within the intimate space of the home and family. When out on the streets, empowered women may fight their own battles, but it is within the family where she lacks an ally in a parent, her in-laws, and often even in her partner. The reported number of domestic violence cases during the lockdown[7] is disheartening proof[8] of the same. Familial spaces presuppose gender inequality which adds to the power hierarchy of heteronormative familial relationships.

There are a few self-reflective pieces in the collection. Alvin Pang's "Lovers without Hands" begins with 'Let's stand in front of mirrors and rehearse touch.' The poem calls for empathy, agency, and mutual pleasure in intimate relations. Chand writes about gender identity with a kind of fierceness that comes only with defying gender binaries. Gender fluidity is a distinct aspect that plays with the readers' minds in Chand's "My Gender," Dibyajyoti Sarma's "In Which Shikhandi Regrets His Decision," K. Satchidanandan's "She, Inside Me," and Ra Sh's "Andro and Estro." These poems strike a necessary balance in an anthology that focuses on harassment and violence against women. Tim Kahl's "An Underdog in Training" and Manik Sharma's "Leaving" discuss the speakers' frailties and fears. Amlanjyoti Goswami's "On the Terrace" explores what Jacques Lacan explains as 'the fear of the father.' Goswami presents a moment in his poem where children deliberate upon inviting the father to play, worrying if he would curtail their spirit. 'The height of your father, waiting. A komodo dragon' is an image that uses 'father' as a symbol that patriarchy often associates with terror, power, and punishment to invoke fear in children.

This anthology responds to various tenets of third and fourth-wave feminism. Feminist theories do not exclude men from its periphery. It must be noted that anti-men statements that are rampant in popular media are misrepresentations of feminist politics. We believe in bell hooks' imagination: "Feminism is for Everybody," or as Chimamanda Ngozi Adichie emphasizes that men should be gender-sensitive[9], or as Kamla Bhasin puts it: 'Feminism is not biological. Feminism is an ideology.'[10] We believe feminism is a way of life and requires instillation in a nation's cultural memory. Men's involvement in feminist politics does not necessarily override women's struggles. Instead, it builds a web of solidarity for empathetic futures.

In recent times, some brilliant series and films have been released that deal with social issues with a kind of empathy that was often lacking in their precursors. For instance, *Criminal Justice: Behind Closed Doors* (2020) and *Pieces of a Woman* (2020) ask difficult questions through their anti-sexist portrayal of female bodies and female experiences of loss. The cinematic depiction of the female body bereft of a male glance (in the shows mentioned above) helps de-glamorize marriage and motherhood. Also, the fact that both the shows have male directors is a hopeful turn for feminist art and politics. In a way, the anthology is inspired by this shift in attitude in mainstream media.

In light of the above statement, it would be good to explore a few pieces from the anthology. Motherhood juxtaposed with deprivation and sacrifice is depicted in Milan Mondal's "The Silent Lane" and Dibyajyoti Sarma's "In Which We Eat." It is refreshing to note that these poems lack the celebratory tone that one connects with motherhood. The old and ailed female body is a common symbol of neglect in our households. The image of the old woman in Sanket Mhatre's "Bed No. 187" indicates how human bodies are weighed against their material and economic value. Female bodies suffer tremendous neglect and disrespect as they move beyond their procreating age. Mhatre writes, 'A night ago, she held my hand and cried—*If I die here, will you take me back to my village?* She handed me a letter with no address.' Quite a few other poems in the collection explore this theme with subtlety. Vivekanand Selvaraj's "Bharat Mata" (translates as 'Mother-India') has an exciting take on hyper-masculine nationalism that perceives a country as a 'motherland' requiring constant protection and preservation. Selvaraj parodies this notion and presents nationalism as mere school performance.

What holds this anthology together is its depiction of cheap sexual labor and unpaid female domestic labor—offerings that patriarchal society thrives on. The poets, through their pieces, blur barriers between the Madonna and the Whore[11]. The collection begins with Abhay K.'s dedication to 'pleasure givers,' who are hurt most by government agents, lawmakers, and executives, who, instead of targeting demand, enable organized crime against sex workers. Abhay K. portrays them as 'pulled into police vans, taxis, limousines and dumped somewhere.' The Madonna is strikingly merged with the Whore in Basab Mondal's "Foetus," as a 'moll,' carrying a child in her dark womb, is accompanied by a 'halo.' Or, as Milan Mondal depicts—mother willing to go with anyone without 'bargaining' so that she may be able to feed her little ones. Sexual slavery is the norm for coolie women in Khal Torabully's extracts from *Voices from Aparavasi Ghat*, for young girls in Amit Shankar Saha's "Trafficked," for home-makers in Paresh Tiwari's "Surviving Marital Rape," or as Ra Sh points out, even for young men in prisons. The latter writes, 'In prison, my ass is a treasure sought after by 1000 men. Catcalls follow me, wolf whistles fly around me, My ass is groped...branded by the owner, emasculated, feminized.' Oppressive social structures enable toxic masculinity. Spaces of work and domesticity become an abstraction of emotional abuse. The female body that is a metaphor for silence, sadness, and burden, paints the walls she lives within with wails of trauma. An impending burden of household chores is thrust upon Sumallya Mukhopadhyay's characters, *Maa* and *Didi*, or the wife in Raja Chakraborty's "Of Houses," or the maids in Abhay K.'s "A Maid's Monologue" and Ankush Banerjee's "Two Women."

Cultural theorists have now moved beyond an ideological understanding of the world to identity politics that pays heed to individual lives and their choices, desires, and necessities. The anthology voices concerns shared by *Dalit*, Indigenous, and Queer poets portraying and celebrating realities that patriarchal society and elected governments have for long invisibilized and ghettoized as non-existent. We believe writing about feminist issues cannot be divorced from one's racial and class identities, and I have done my very best to incorporate varied voices that discuss the same.

I often wonder: Now that women are speaking up, are we willing to listen? The scope of no feminist movement is ever limited to only calling out heteropatriarchal[12] violence. Instead, they aim at bringing back the promised safety into this world. We must move beyond visualizing feminist men *only* as leaders[13], and now they should be able to inhabit our everyday lives. This collection is merely a beginning. It hopes to achieve at least something of what it aims at: developing and promoting a feminist conscience in a society fraught with violence and regressive politics.

SHAMAYITA SEN
May 2021
New Delhi

[1] from Judith Butler's *Gender Trouble* (1990)

[2] an Indian classical dance form

[3] Tarana Burke began using the phrase "Me Too" in 2006 to raise awareness of women who had been abused. In 2017, the movement found global recognition after a viral tweet by actress Alyssa Milano.

[4] Khal Torabully uses heteroglossia as a means to challenge monolingual perceptions of language and identity.

[5] quote from bell hooks' *Feminism is for Everybody: Passionate Politics* (2000)

[6] normalization of heterosexual practices

[7] Lockdown was declared in various countries to contain Covid-19.

[8] The UN has described the worldwide increase in domestic abuse as a 'shadow pandemic' alongside Covid-19.

[9] inferred from Chimamanda Ngozi Adichie's speech, "We should all be feminists." (*TEDxEuston*, April 2013)

[10] from Kamla Bhasin's conversation with Lilinaz Evans and Hannah Pool (*New Internationalist*, July-August, 2014)

[11] A reference to the Madonna-Whore Complex. Patriarchal setups perceive women in either of the two categories: the Madonna or the Whore. The Madonna is a de-sexualised figure of women as the Mother, as against the explicitly sexualised figure of the Whore. And, for the tragedy of the society, these two categories are not meant to overlap in most fiction, even though in real life, most women house both characteristics within themselves.

[12] enabling the authority of cisgender male and heterosexuals over people of other genders and sexual orientation

[13] To name a few prominent Indian social activists in this context: Raja Rammohan Roy (eradication of Sati and abolition of child marriage), Iswar Chandra Vidyasagar (widow remarriage and female education), B. R. Ambedkar (Hindu Code Bill).

ACKNOWLEDGMENTS

Through the many discussions we have had of the failing society, of personal losses, of broken hearts, I believe I have formed solidarity with friends and colleagues and have moved a step closer to creating an empathetic future and finding allies even amidst political turmoil. This is to acknowledge each such friendship. Through our sharing of personal trauma and details of failed relationships, we have taught each other techniques to survive this world marred by toxic masculinity.

I lived in a hostel in Delhi when the Me Too movement began (in 2017). I remember having conversations about the mind-numbing stress and disbelief that follow sexual harassment. Even before the Me Too movement happened, I remember discussing sexual misconduct with my hostel-mates—my friends. They were no less than family then, now authors, educators, and young professionals in their own right. Much of the person I am today can be attributed to Adrija Roychowdhury, Srishti Sahu, Urmi Bhattacheryya, Pragya Anurag, and Suman Bhagchandani.

I extend my gratitude to fellow poets, academics, and friends, Rajorshi Das, Semeen Ali, Nikita Parik, Anindita Ghosh, and Arpita Sarker, for encouraging and enlightening me. Discussions with them have helped me widen the scope of this anthology. This project would not have been possible without their constant help and inputs. I am highly thankful to Sanjeev Sethi, Chandramohan Sathyanathan, and Aswin Vijayan for connecting me to poets and allies in India and abroad, who I then solicited submissions from. Poets from all over the country and various parts of the world, including the US, England, South Africa, UAE, China, Singapore, Pakistan, and Italy, responded to this open call for poems.

The book wouldn't have been possible had it not been for the forty-four poets who had contributed to the project, who have responded timely to all my mails. I can't thank *Hawakal Publishers* enough to believe in my work and vision and invest in this project. Their constant support and scaffolding have made my journey smooth and enjoyable. I shall forever be grateful to Professor Saikat Majumdar for investing his valuable time into writing a beautiful foreword that speaks volumes about the collection.

Finally, I thank my parents and maternal grandparents—my feminist role models—for providing me opportunities and avenues that have helped me open my mind, shun judgment, and revere alternate cultures as equally relevant. I owe much of this also to my liberal education and upbringing. I specifically miss *Baba* and *Dida* today as I write this. I wish I could read this collection with them. I know in my heart they would have enjoyed reading these poems just as much. My partner has often exemplified what feminist men must be like. Having him around makes me hopeful for our generation.

Here's hoping that the anthology will reach out to more readers than we expect, that it will inspire and influence its readers. Here's also hoping to see future editions of the anthology.

POETS

ABHAY K.

Mysterious Lady Of Konark

The tree is happy because it is scarcely sentient; / the hard rock is happier still, it feels nothing. – Ruben Dario

At the Sun Temple in Konark stone sculptures make love to each other ignoring the voyeurs. Centuries have passed. Her nose is gone, her hands are broken, her body has cracks, and her breasts have withered. She has stoically borne glare of sun and caress of moon. She has withstood cyclones and storms. Corrosive sea winds have made her skin rough. She has been physically assaulted by the invaders, the raiders of ancient sculptures, smugglers. She has handled unwanted attention. She has dealt with capricious officials, whimsical politicians and narcissists. She does not look stressed even a bit. She has kept her infectious smile.

ABHAY K.

The Pleasure Givers

I see you standing in Thamel, Sukhumbit, Le Paquis
in pleasure lanes of Savay Pak, Point Road, Kamaliya
in the red light districts of Dashilan, DeVallen, the Deuce
wearing heavy make-up, in tacky clothes

looking anxiously into your tiny mirrors
waiting for someone to stop and smile
I see you standing in Simalu, Sonagachi, Rose Street
in every season as it is always spring

I see you pulled into police vans, taxis, limousines
and dumped somewhere in Kabukicho, King's Cross,
Koinange, disheveled, bleeding
I see you at G.B. Road, Geylang, Halmtorvet,

combing your hair, colouring your lips,
lining your eyes, careening yourself
at Oranienburger, Barrio Chino or Vivian Street
occasionally throwing a slant glance at someone approaching.

Today I see an empty spot at Heera Mandi, Chow Kit,
Rue de Aerschot Mira-ri, Gurtel, Kamathipura,
for days where you always stood waiting
perhaps you're at a hospital recovering

or in your village visiting your relatives
or at your rented shack resting in darkness
or perhaps rotting in a prison
or serving policemen.

I see your soul being strangled every hour
I see you drinking hemlock as Socrates
I see you kissing death with your golden lips.
The pleasure-givers, I see you.

ABHAY K.

A Maid's Monologue

I am your djinn,
I am your angel
I am your house help
I am nobody, I am your maid.

I am a Latino, I am a Filipino
I am a Nepali, I am a Uzbek
I am an Indian, I am a Caribbean
I am an African, I am a Burmese

I am a Chinese, I am a Pakistani
I am every nation on the Earth.
I polish your shoes, I wash your clothes
I clean your house, I cook your food

I press your garments,
I look after your children,
I shop your groceries
I give you every comfort.

I live in windowless holes
I eat leftovers from the kitchen

I sleep on the floor
I am first to rise, I am last to sleep

I work seven days a week
Without any break
I am always at your beck and call
I don't celebrate festivals

I speak your language in smatterings
I only listen, you speak
I am dumb-witted, I'm a half-alive robot
I am a still-born Cinderella.
I am a cuckoo that can't sing
I am a swan that can't swim
I am a tiger that can't roar
I am an eagle that can't fly

I am without a past and future
I am merely present.
I live unloved
I am an easy prey for you

my breasts ever ready to be suckled
my words—my silence.
My passport forfeited
my earnings withheld

my body sick, my hands rough
my feet full of cracks
my shoes old, my clothes torn.
I am chained to your monstro-city

back home, someone waits
on the deathbed
to be fed, to be bathed, to be cured.
Someone waits for my last glimpse.

ADITYA SHANKAR

The Old Woman's Kitchen

Has grown feeble like an old throat.
A space aware of the strain of noise and pace.
Neighbourhood cats are braver here, lounging on the slab.
The wrinkled hands, kinder, offering an extra fish.
Beneath the knife those hands hold,
It seems the vegetables are no more chopped,
But patted to the meditation of an eternal sleep.
Pressure cooker, telling, in the way it fizzles out.
A single dish simmers laboriously, as if a feast,
Yet satiates an old hunger, now wiser like a saint.
Like a grave that steadily buries itself in soil and weed,
Dirt takes over the rims of her casseroles and tumblers.
Maybe death arrives this way, earthly and hushed.

ALAN BRITT

Blue

She wore blue; she wore whatever the
world saw through & donated as hand-
me-downs for the next generation.

She didn't know, exactly, how to break
the cycle, though she knew she wanted to.

ALAN BRITT

Myth Of The Baker's Daughter

They say the owl
used to be a baker's daughter
with wild hyacinth hair.

As a matter of fact,
people were barely able to detect any color
at all in her flowing hair.

Her legs were smoke,
although many believed she consisted entirely
of water.

She spent much time pleasing & nurturing,
as you would expect from a baker's daughter.

This went on for several thousand years.
Her life-span was a drop of quicksilver.

Then came the day when her services
no longer pleased;
the world had completely forgotten her.

Eventually, the world created a new job for her,
though. It now needed her to clean rodents
from death's teeth.

But she endured.

Over the course of time,
perhaps several more millennia,
the world lost
complete control
over her muscular arms,
& without warning
her arms evolved into bronze feathers.

Tonight, on the cool branch of a midnight pine,
sits an owl
who used to be a baker's daughter.

ALLAN KOLSKI HORWITZ

Bringing Forth

Eve was there
alone
she had no need for another
she was full-breasted

and she lay in the garden
seeding herself
and her milk made her happy
Eve after Eve after Eve

but when the moon was full and red
a warring rod and whirling light
disturbed her womb
till a hard-muscled child pulsed out

so Eve made Adam
made herself and unmade herself
made a man to stand
beside and against her

it is never quiet in the garden
there is always vibration
and still Eve lies alone
bringing forth Adam after Adam after Adam

ALLAN KOLSKI HORWITZ

Census

They came to the shelter for battered women
enumerators in orange t-shirts
they came to fill forms
to ask and record

and the battered women peered out
from behind their bruises their blemishes
peered out with sour looks and grimaces
and touching their welts and their scars
stumbled from their beds
shuffled out of the TV-room
crawled out from the cracks

the battered women in the shelter
came out to give answers
confirm bare facts
so proud to be reckoned alive
among those whose needs
need to be written down
researched made allowance for

standing in front of the enumerators
it was almost like being famous
this being counted as if you count

ALVIN PANG

Lovers Without Hands

Let's stand in front of mirrors and rehearse
touch, a time of drupe we did not know

to conserve. Now your sheen's dry heat scours
the sweep, daunts pour. There is no need

to hide from dead roses, their thorns don't reach
as deep as scarlet, the dip of pen into blotch.

Now we have a love that does not scar;
your skin parchment only to forgetting

and already, damp with time, you are tearing
like the arc of a wave seen from a star

incurious to origins. When you come
to my shore will you put on your nakedness

or will you, shy of rue, guise in wanting?
Distance becomes horizon. The glass between us

misty with breath. Our story becomes landscape
to the life we give way to: we are travelled,

arrived at, unplumbed lagoons reliving the sweet
blue else. I ask nothing. Wait with me.

AMAL JOSEPH MATHEW

An Ode To Woolf
14.41

"When I find myself in times of trouble, Mother Mary comes to me
Speaking words of wisdom, let it be"

A painter recalls   the face of God.
Pulling her temple across the wall
                              she piques at climax.

Across the wall are paintings. Paintings in her house
watch her sleep. Slouching about the fingers
of beautiful girls, she picked off the phonebook.

Girls with names of flowers
                              or   handicapped passages.
If she is able to open their palms, they go birdwatching
by the pier, offering peace to the side-walks,
the posters, the latticed mosque walls.

Before religion, her vanishing act included glass tables,
elective English, the daily columns.

Seahorses
danced
into
the break of light. The male, bearing life, facing
the lap of the ocean.
In twenty-four days, he will begin to hope.
Unlike the other parent, *much obliged.*

And hope is dangerous, when it comes to love—
seemingly average in its approach.
The hooded sympathy of warmongers.

Those who preach love are average,
they love average.
Remain wary of them, they do not understand the ways
of birds, or images, or women returning from work.

*

They are impatient. They want to run, before they crawl. Finish,
before they start.
On the altar, she prays to the paintings of girls
on their knees. Awakening their thighs.
Perhaps mouthing behind the riddels, an earnest prayer for penitence.
the church condemns suicide a sin
Even in partial remission, one remains floating.

Photosynthesis begins at partial daybreak, a safer survival.
The shrubs in Massachusetts do not preach love, they do not,
they do not.
They accommodate hatred for preachers,
remain wary of them. Plants understand better—the ways
of ornithology or photography or women walking into the Ouse,
with stones in their pockets, calling it madness.

The painter recalls the face of God; it is a woman.

AMIT SHANKAR SAHA

Trafficked

I undress
as I write this.
There goes the last
thread from my body.
In the corners
of every room
I shed a sigh
of missing girls,
who are supposed
to be long dead.
Between the furrows
of the fields
my eyes roam.
Greens become gray
far away.
Fertility consorts
with the rich loam.
When it's pitch dark
you can see us

amidst the ploughshares.
Patrols screech
at my naked borders,
search all my moans.
I beg for some shame.
When will I be home?

AMIT SHANKAR SAHA

The Outsider

On World Valentine's Day
I decide to write a feminist poem.
I imagine myself like a woman,
oppressed and depressed,
who has escaped the oven,
who stirs her imagination within utensils,
pastes it on tins of provisions,
colours it with her menstrual blood,
hides it behind nights of unconsent,
I imagine my imagination
stunted by language of power,
and all the words I birth
become husbands and fathers,
I imagine my imagination
struggling within bellies and breasts,
I imagine my imagination
suffocating behind eyelids of unrest,
until it congeals into a tumour in my head.
I cannot write a feminist poem
for my mother is dead.

AMLANJYOTI GOSWAMI

The Day After

The river is wed.
She is leaving her mother
Tonight

Mother muffles a tear
Says you are marrying
Moha bahu Brahmaputra

Of the strong arms and warm embrace.
She nods, but knows
She likes her little stream better.

The stream she spends
            her afternoon quiet,
With mud banks, sunlit alleys

  Silver flying fishes.
The stream who listens to her
  and keeps all her little secrets.

AMLANJYOTI GOSWAMI

On The Terrace

We tiptoed, on white marble
An inch at a time, carefully dodging the monsters
Those little creatures, bugs and bees.

We passed a snake or two, said hello to wood ducks
About to take off for Siberia
Where they came from winter.

Peered at a monkey on a plank
Sailing away from the crocodile.
Fishes of every colour. Sharks, piranhas

Magur, rou. Worms wriggling beneath the rushes.
Waters trembling as we sailed slowly,
Holding hands, not letting go.

Our boat far from destination—
The other side, where a black door lay.
We saw tiny crocodiles all around—

Scaly, not yet ripe to bite,
Looking like things you could carry on your palm.
We thought better about it.

There were others, more dangerous.
One more step, there it was, in front—
The height of your father, waiting.

A komodo dragon, all the way from Indonesia.
We wondered which tack would work, a handshake
To welcome him to the party or maybe, Bruce Lee kicks for free?

Who should make the first move? You said
He looked like the friendly dinosaur next door,
The one you sometimes invite for dinner.

AMMAR AZIZ

An Ode To Nightingales

I thought my mother was hurt
When I saw her blood
Soaked pads in trash—
The five year old me
Was shocked

And once when father
Beat her up
For something mundane
I never thought
She was in pain
Though I saw her scars

Because that's how
All fathers treated
All mothers
In that town

Where women
Often became nightingales
Disappearing into the stars.

Note: This is not culled out of personal experiences.

ANKUSH BANERJEE

Two Women

My grandmother's family home
was an absurd boulder
thirty miles from the border.[1]
It had country dogs trained to conjure intruders
from pond and mustard fields.
In summers the siblings stayed indoors, ate mangoes,
moulding themselves into the afternoon-listlessness
of pockmarked villages. In the slush and mud of monsoons,
they tied dead crickets, ants, grasshoppers
to stones that carelessly hop the water's surface
one, two, three, four, plop.

Except one monsoon when the stone
went—one, two, three—four was a limp body of a girl
they pulled out from the water,
the ant-tied-stone stuck in her open mouth.
No one knew how to administer CPR.
The siblings played hopscotch on her bulging chest, until
lungs gurgled green pond-water and hope. They named
her with bloodstones of affections

dredged from the gut: *Tor daak naam Kalindi.*[2]

When I ask *thamma*[3]
where Kalindi the maid came from,
or why they ate from similar plates, she beams
as a girl rejoicing in her one deciding game
of hopscotch. *I restrained the dogs*
from biting her face—is a
sentence she unpeels from memory,
drawing parallels from her history class—
like Albert Battel, the Nazi Officer who saved an
insignificant but certain number of Jews.[4]

*

In family albums, I find my great-grandfather scowling,
nervous, moustachioed men fussing
over *that* bastard girl they call *jol er dayon*,[5]
while my thirteen-year-old grandmother fasted,
punishing her body
for the hole
that lie in her family's heart.
Her oesophagus congealed like earthworms
in the wizened surface
of the pond in summers. On the fourth day,
the family relents, lest heart-hole become
a black-hole of remorse. Both girls were fed
from the same plate.

Now, when I tell her that Kalindi
often washes and uses the same plate
grandmother eats in,
she, at eighty-three, smiles as if she is thirteen,
standing on the rooftop of her village home,

pointing a finger to the border,
and telling dear Kalindi—*love and home—*
both are skills. Only one you learn now. The other you learn gradually.

So, choose wisely, my dear.

[1] India-Bangladesh border
[2] Bengali for, 'Your nickname is Kalindi.'
[3] Bengali for paternal grandmother
[4] Albert Battel was a Lieutenant in the German Army during World War II. He was one of the few Germans who resisted the realization of Hitler's 'Final Solution.' When soldiers from the German SS arrived at Przemysl, Poland in July 1942, to launch their first large-scale 'resettlement' program, Battel, a Lieutenant stationed there, not only stopped them, but also ensured that around hundred Jews were sheltered from deportation to the gas chambers. He was posthumously recognised as *Righteous Among the Nations* in 1981.
[5] translates as 'water-witch.'

BASAB MONDAL

Foetus

The half-eaten moon climbs past
the wires of the tram line
to settle in a corner.

Rays from the street light
whitens the penumbra of the city.

The moll carrying the unborn
in the dark of her womb,
alights the last bus.

It halts below the lamp
for the day.

From an obtuse height, the glow
accompanies her like a halo
while she walks through the mist.

BIBHU PADHI

All Through The Long Night

Your quick, considerate light
plays on my skin.

As the night grows into a darker life,
my world acquires a narrow, emphatic heat.

New forces, subtle fields of energy
create themselves between skin and skin
and hold us together in a dear gesture.

But in due time,
a thin flame within you

starts burning through the night.
It dances inside my brain,
deep below my skin.

As the night turns thin and weak,
your defeating red is all there is.

Your small body wins.

BOUDHAYAN MUKHERJEE

Elegy

I crawl numb fingers to locate
my dead child
draped in darkness
inside my unfledged womb.

I don't shriek as my parents have
turned paler than my anaemic skin.

Antiseptic nurses, glassy eyed,
fidget with diapers unused.
The morning is long, longer
than I have lived.
The air is hotter
than I have ever felt before.
I want my partner now
to kiss my forehead.

But he has stayed away.

I don't cry as I have time
left for it—Oh! hollow hours,
without my child.

CHAND

My Gender

My gender is a crown of thorns.
Of course, it doesn't fit in your binaries of man and woman.
It smells of rose and jasmine
And hot steaming black coffee sipped slowly at dusk.
It was chiselled by taunts of sissy
And *gandu* and *chakka*.
It was baked in the oven of shame
But trust me, the frosting is super sweet.
My gender is steeped in love,
Warmth and utopian fantasies
That coalesce into collective aspirations.
It is still reverberating sometimes with their snickers
Their malicious lies and gossip.
My gender drapes itself in a red Pochampally *saree* really well,
Not to forget multi-coloured flared palazzos,
It totally rocks the *bindi* and *kajal* look.
My gender tastes like butter chicken at times,
And like Banoffee pie on other occasions.
My gender is cast in euphoria,

Shaped by the resistance to the forces that bind us.
My gender runs wild, a river in spate,
Flowing through your dams of screening committees
And binary citizenship registers.
It laughs at the idea that you could tame it.
My gender fucks with your mind and categories
And wants to fuck you.
My gender makes me happy.

CHANDRAMOHAN SATHYANATHAN

On Inter-Caste Love

Just like the saying goes—
The tongue has no bones
But can break many,

The submissive tuft of hair
On the shaven heads
Of the twice-born
Command an army of henchmen
Guarding the rust
Of medieval fences built
Along caste-hymens.

Two love poems
From two different languages
Elope on a moonless night
Storming the Bastille
Of "apparently impregnable fortresses"
Of their syntax.

CHANDRAMOHAN SATHYANATHAN

Plus-Sized Poem

This poem refuses to be
The world's wife.

This poem is not pimple-free,
Is printed on rough paper.

This poem has cellulite in its rear end,
Its rump out-sizes itself off the market.

This poem walks the ramp with a self-edited gait
Without introduction or foreword from veterans.

This poem does not opt for offshore liposuction
To make oneself eligible for international prizes.

This poem eludes the trap
In the hourglass of time.

CHANDRAMOHAN SATHYANATHAN

Portrait Of A Poet As A Young Woman

Her hair—
freshly harvested dreadlocks,
unedited gospel of love,
off limits to combs.

Tresses stream
like eternal fire
from the arsenal of her body.

Poems conceived in a celestial tongue
when stars align with caesarean precision—
it is our own language.

Her verses
are neither left nor right-aligned.
Time zones hinge at every line break
like sunflowers unaligned to the scorching heat.

Every evening, on her terrace,
she lets down her hair and flies a kite;

her verses tell vivid stories
stitched together in myriad colours.

Her verses gurgle like rivers let loose.
She never braids them
before a poetry reading.

When her poems are read
no boyfriend or pimp is allowed
inside the reading hall.

Her kite, untethered to her surname,
soars high, till it gets entangled with the stars.

Attempting to translate her poems
is like making love to a capricious mistress.

Her curly, kinky stream of verses
sway to the rhythm of her gait
untamed by the clanging of her anklets.

Her book of poems
is a treatise on disheveled hair
and tresses on fire.

Black women are often not *considered as objects of desire in films. And they have always been my core audience.* – Denzel Washington on refusing to lip-lock with Julia Roberts.

The wild flowers that bloom and die in Challapali are Dalit *women—scholars and intellectuals included—who fade and die unappreciated.* – Challapalli Swaroopa Rani

DEBARSHI MITRA

Genesis

Even as I walked there
by the sea
that raged on soundless
rising as if from the very depths
of our being
or un-being,
I thought I knew
the unborn sons
and the unborn daughters
that lay there
eternally dreaming,
will not be woken up,
the endless capillaries
of blood will not spill,
will not be casualties
of countless wars, will not
lay down familial bonds,
they will flow along
like a latent river

of unheard stories,
their courses
uncharted, untraced.
Just as a thought,
a possibility
of life merging with light
on a spring day,
waiting for you
to remember them
from the endless expanse
of your memory,

waiting for you
to call them
by their names.

DIBYAJYOTI SARMA

In Which We Eat

1.
Have the last morsel, Yajnaseni. The vessel is empty.
Everything has been shared.
The husbands are content.
The sons have gone back to sleep;
the daughters wait.
Mother, have the last morsel; the vessel is empty.
Outside the guests gather.
Mother, nurture us.
What would you do, Yajnaseni?
Cook your flesh? Cook the flesh of your daughters?
A tumbler full of your tears cannot quench their thirst.
The embers of your eyes cannot light the kitchen fire, mother.
Cook your flesh!
Cook the flesh of your daughters!
Your sons are asleep, your husbands content.
Outside, the guests gather, starved.
Have the last morsel, Yajnaseni; the vessel is empty.

2.
This grain of rice.
This is where it begins.
This is where it ends.
This grain of rice.
The husk is for birds.
The peeled skin is for animals.
The gruel is for reptiles.
This grain of rice.
Have the last morsel, Yajnaseni;
the vessel is empty.

3.
This last morsel is for the boy who hasn't smelt a balloon.
This last morsel is for the girl who hasn't seen a pencil.

4.
This grain is for the impotent father of three unmarried daughters.
This drop of lentil is for the rickshaw-puller under the rain.
This pod of peas is for the cobbler on the footpath where no one walks.
This piece of *sandesh* is for the old woman who cleans the lavatory.
This fish scale is for the farmer whose sons went to the raging sea.
This piece of bone is for the butcher who lost his family in the riot.
This peel of onion is for the leader to cry crocodile tears.
This drop of blood is for the soldier outside no man's land.
This neem leaf is for the revolutionary awaiting his end in a dark cell.
These wild mushrooms are for everyone who wants to start over.
And this vessel is for you, Yajnaseni. The vessel is empty.

5.
Everything is empty,
the sky is empty of water,
the earth of green leaves.

Our bellies empty of food,
        our minds of hope.

6.
This last morsel is for Jayanta Mahapatra
who would share it with the old fisherman.

Note: During their time in exile, as guests always visit the Pandavs, and as royal hosts, as they are duty-bound to invite guests to eat with them; and as *Draupadi*, the designated cook, doesn't have the resources to feed so many people, she implores Annapurna, the goddess of food, and receives a copper vessel. The catch? The vessel would offer unending supply of food as long as *Draupadi* doesn't eat. Once she has eaten, the vessel is empty until the next morning when she cooks again.

DIBYAJYOTI SARMA

In Which Ganga Explains

I too dream,
not like lovers, giddy, exhaustive daydreams,
not like ambitious fathers,
not like alley cats dreaming of fish,
not like highway truck drivers dreaming of beds.
I dream like rivers do, of things lost, irretrievable,
I dream of the past,
a history of time incalculable—
these days, I mostly dream of
dead turtles and crocodiles.

Not the future, which is foretold, the end will arrive,
I dream of the past that glitters
like a thousand stars on a summer night,
the past that did not die; my past and yours,
and His with Matted Hair,
His with Peacock Feathers,
his with the shaven head,
his with the sacred thread,

and his sons and grandsons,
the past of kings and killers.

Like a rag that cleans the floor,
once my glittering attire woven in water,
the past is lost. I'm what is forgotten,
like the beggar woman who once had a home.

And I'm free to roam the earth,
to collect shards of broken memories,
to count specks of ashes.

I dream like mothers do,
of their offspring's future.
I forget my dream and dream yours.
I weep at your demise,
as I will for generations after you.
Like a patient mother I make you forget,
and I remember.

I'm the despair that gives you hope.

I'm the mother of all that is forgotten,
of dead things, filth...

I'm the mother of this very existence,
these lines, dry ink.

I'm the mother of drowned babies,
suicidal virgins, fallen soldiers, lustful widows.

I'm the mother of decrepit bodies,

mango barks, sandalwood,
of dirt, of fire...

I'm the mother of everything that decays,
of boats and roots, of rain
and the waning moon.

Note: *Ganga* descended to *Mrityulok* to free the ancestors of Prince Bhagirath. Yet, she is destined to remain earth-bound until the end of time, until everything is over and the world ceases to spin.

DIBYAJYOTI SARMA

In Which Shikhandi Regrets His Decision

It's good to be a human, Parth, preferably a man. You know that,
being a prince, and being loved, and being safe in the knowledge.
It's good to be a god too, Madhusudhan, you know that,
you remember nothing, since you forget nothing. Consider me,
then, in this body of flesh and bone I do not recognise.

And the memories this body cannot comprehend. You say I'm
my father's son, but I remember another father, whose daughter
I was. You say, he's just an old man, *Pitamah*, but I remember
a young archer, uncouth, and heartless, who'd listen to no one,
but his own voice. I blink, and I'm someone else.

And now, on the threshold of my goal, for which I have navigated
two births, two lives, and sacrificed everything human—love, family,
and that insatiable desire to leave my mark on stone columns,
I have but one regret. I did not live out my life. After all,
I was a princess and he was not the only man.

He knows, you say, I'm a woman, but Madhusudhan, I am not. My soul may be, but not my body; this I crafted myself through tears of desolate childhood of neither being a boy nor a girl, neither being loved nor loathed, and I have endured a thousand lonely nights waiting for this day. Now my heart beats for him and he wouldn't face me.

Oh, Parth, it's time to end this endless quest, so perhaps I could learn to live after he was dead, and experience desire other than for this old man who created a kingdom over his unyielding torso, which is now obsessed with its destruction, as I was once, and all I have now is just one regret; that in the end, I became the same man I so deliriously despised.

Note: Shikhandi, Arjun's other brother-in-law, wants to fight and kill Bhishm during the war. But on the eve of the crucial battle, he is informed by Krishn and Arjun that the patriarch wouldn't fight him because he remembers Shikhandi's past life as the princess of Kashi, Amba, whom he abducted and then spurned (long story!); because he had vowed he wouldn't raise arms against women. Now, Krishn wants Shikhandi to ride in Arjun's chariot as a human shield so that the old man would drop his weapon and the warrior of our age would finally kill him.

DURGA PRASAD PANDA

Her Body

Sometimes, in the dense darkness
of the night she stretches her hands
and tries to touch her body

lying somewhere far away from her.
Throughout her life she goes on
searching for that ever elusive body,

a body she would have wrapped around
herself like a warm piece of blanket
through the long winter nights

of her loneliness. She knows for sure
that her body alone
is her ultimate refuge.

She wonders where will she keep hiding
this damned body of her.
It seems to have no respite at all!

If it escapes the quagmire,
the fire waits to swallow her up.
If it escapes the raging flame,

a river sweeps her away.
When she drops all her inhibitions,
the market drags her into its clutches.

If she escapes the jabbed fangs
of the market, a lusty priest
pounces upon her.

Carrying this hell of a body,
in the darkness of broad daylight,
even if she wishes to,

where exactly will she go?

Translated from the Odia by the poet.

DUSTIN PICKERING

Ritual Potential

too many mouth wormwood
gunned from the Machiavellian tongue
                    of ancient error

rather than embrace
ritual potential
                    of women warriors

DUSTIN PICKERING

Untitled

for Evan Rachel Wood

darkness follows you
tearing holes in your silence

while cobwebs star his ceiling,
a fathomless ego-abyss.

GOIRICK BRAHMACHARI

As I Watch The Road

A girl lights her cigarettes
and smokes out her disgust
onto faces of four coughing men
who watch her
as if she is naked.
Old grandmothers
in Neb Sarai smoke pot
when the day is done.
A kid lights a stick and burns dendrite
to fight hunger and a hot summer.
A construction worker
lights her *bidi*
before stacking twenty bricks
onto her head. No one questions her
right to smoke at the end of a tiring day.

GOPAL LAHIRI

Dark Reservoir

A sycamore tree reminds how I used to be weak.
The dark alleyway sends my unexpressed desires
until it needles into the crust, into the bone.

Walking against the sorrow, grief, sadness
I register burnt flesh and split arteries in black board.
The night punches through the city's thickest skin.

Old coffee-house evokes memory, a kind of index
for our turbulent life, drums in day and night
living on the bare, love letters get splattered at the burner.

The extent of misery, the frightful abeyance erases.
A cloud sweep over a cornfield, records the transition,
detain in a dream-world of longing, solitude, candour.

Keeping me awake the ever-rising orange flame
as if half-dead becomes half-alive,
between you and me, masculine rage and ineffable sanity.

INAM HUSSAIN BEGG MULLICK

Fear Of Lizards

She remembers the teacher
as he crawled into the class,

and looks at the door
in the haze of the blue lamp,

far away the fire-wagon
rings upon the owl,

and interrupts the tree;

she coils in bed
like an overcast prayer,

the rat recognizes the ghost,

that teacher had talked
of a mathematics
of unlocked doors,

somewhere
a singer curses his own tongue,

she puts off the lamp,

the fan spins
like a ritual of blood,

on the streets a man vomits,

she tries to sleep,

the fire-wagon tolls every year
this day,

the cockroach holds
on to the darkness
of the wall,

she feels the singer's pain,
and trembles

at the noise
of a brother,

the lizard brings good luck.

K. SATCHIDANANDAN

Non-Negotiable

She stripped herself bare
and scrawled with charcoal
all over her body: 'non-negotiable.'

Then she poured petrol
from head to foot
and set herself afire.

K. SATCHIDANANDAN

Burnt Poems

I am a half-burnt poem.
Yes, you guessed right,
a girl's love poem.

Girls' love poems have
seldom escaped fire:
father's fire, brother's fire,
even mother's, an heirloom.

Only some girls half-escape:
those half-charred ones
we call Sylvia Plath,
Anna Akhmatova
or Kamala Das.

Some girls, to escape fire,
hide their desire
under the veil of piety:
thus is born a Meera,

an Andal, a Mahadevi Akka.

Every nun is a burnt
love-poem, addressed to
the ever-young Jesus.

Rarely, very rarely,
one girl learns to
laugh at the world
with that tender affection
only women are capable of.
Then the world names her
Wislawa Szymborska.

Of course, Sappho:
she was saved only as
her love poems were
addressed to women.

K. SATCHIDANANDAN

She, Inside Me

As a child I used to dance
in front of the mirror
in skirt and bangles.
That girl is still dancing inside me.
I conceal her with my hair,
man's voice and attire.

But at times she leaps out,
breaking every shell,
longing to be addressed as
mother and sister and daughter,
tempting me to befriend
women more than men,
leaving me wondering
whether what I feel
towards some men is just
friendship or intimate love,
being persecuted, resisting,
taking over the anger and tears of

child-brides, widows, prostitutes,
and slain women and
cursing the world of men.

I would have danced in squares
had I not been scared
of men's stoning.

Abuse me saying I am
neither man nor woman:
I reject gender; God
doesn't have one.
But I refuse to be used as a cover
for a coward to kill an old man.[1]

[1] Arjuna, the Mahabharata hero hid behind Shikhandi to kill Bhishma.

KHAL TORABULLY

Voices From The Aapravasi Ghat
excerpts

I
I am woman deposed
In a depot of *dhobis*

In a *ghat* of coolies….

II
Then I became a police case
About rape resistance and coolie chase

Bruises and abuses of female conscription
I waited longer than my menstrual circle[1]
Deposed and proposed at the depot

He then shouted as cyclone over masts:
Get to your ghat you guts of bomlass!
He the roaring constable sweating in his threats.
…

My quota is higher than my *lota*
They square me in a small *samosa*

Gotta tell you how my depot
Attached me to walls and shadows of demise

Hey Police-wallah, where is a woman first abused?
In her head or in her heart? In her flesh?

In her mind, in her memory: in her silence!
But who can hear my silence?

III
Then I answered to the white Sahib's hearing:

Got married during voyage Sahib
Waves fell on me
Foam fell on me
Storm crawled on me—
Men of all blue eyes like jelly
Crawled on poor me.

My navel went besides my belly
So I opened my eyes burning with their cruelty:
I will unravel my history
As the first parchment of vanity.
But who will write my plight
For truth and undaunted virginity?

This means getting nearer your quarter
Getting nearer the other half
The half that is exiled forever in you
Poor soul poor coolie poor thing…

IV
The enquirer inquired
From the Queen's own office:
Britannia rules the waves
And I'm only poorhumanfoam
Resisting dispersion and plankton.

Not yet a diaspora but only indentured
Tooth against booth
Nail against hell and hair upon tooth
India reversed, revulsed in my vulva.

Arkati and Mestri said them voices:

So status of female coolies is far from female slaves?
How can an object of Desire be a subject of Empire?
How Sahib?

How can I be freer than a woman?
I mean a coolie and colonized woman from a paria subcontinent?
Twice subjected in this dominion.

[1]The author uses 'circle' instead of 'cycle' as a play on words, to refer to recurrent abuse of women in exploitative labour systems

These poems are excerpts from Khal Torabully's *Voices from the Aapravasi Ghat*. The author re-voices the coolie women who are as audacious as the men who crossed the dark waters, to be indentured. Their memories are to be cherished through their own voices, which, in poetic humility, the poet of coolitude brings from limbo.

KINSHUK GUPTA

Our Sisters In The Garden

smile at the supple shafts of grass, make dunes from mud, carve
windows in it, and call it home. Soaked in sweat, they pluck

weeds, watch cows roaming, ropes trespassing their nostrils,
traces of freckled noon over their smooth backs. Smoothness:

patches of desire folded between their thighs. When the sun
reaches the top of their heads, thinning their shadows

into twigs, they plow their fingers between those wraps
to feel the rats sprint on their backs. They want their bodies

to answer, the way a tendril curls around a stem. When a bird flock
fans in the sky, someone grabs them by strings and drags them

to the stage. They lie flat—a straight row of stones, hear the rattle
of the metal buckle, friction between the leather straps and a snake

sneaks into their sandal-orchard while they imagine their ankles against the sharp tips of grass blades. The next morning, they are dumped

back into the garden, their strings taut. Tired of running away, they wait with stitched tongues for their turn. Wait for their gods to answer.

For waiting is how you dissolve the anguish of getting churned in the snake's stomach. The metal fingers are busy choosing puppets for the next show.

KINSHUK GUPTA

How Our Sisters Live And Die
for Dr. Priyanka Reddy and all others

1
Winter is the season of women coming out
from their *burkhas* to their lovers waiting in a park,
winter is the season of cold backs of couples
pressed against each other during long nights,
winter is the season of our sisters falling down
like cricket stumps. They are painted in red
of vows, gift wrapped in *salwar-kameez* to serve
as *chai-pakora* to the groom's family, jeweled
with necklaces that tighten every time
they dare to look into their father's eyes.

2
The goddess in front of whom we bow our heads
always sits near the feet of their husbands.
Their voices unnoticed as ticking of a clock, skin, white as milk,
bodies wrapped in red *saree* with golden border.
In the multiple hands we make, we give them rusted weapons.

3
The sisters in our neighborhood cycle off to work.
Their faces half covered with threat, another half draped in *chunni.*
Medicine is her second religion.
                She can't ditch the Gods she prays to.
So, she works late nights brushing off her father's fear.
Then one night, she comes curled—
muscles tensed in revolt,
the adjectives of her beauty erased.

4
The political sergeants will come to your homes—
click pictures with your gnarled father to muster votes,
give jobs to your brothers and pension to your mother,
raise placards, light candles, march to India Gate,
before turning a cold shoulder
                until the same repeats again.

You come in my dreams to say how you want your mother
to stop thinking that your breasts are hanging
stones and ask your father to swell his chest,
for you fought till your breath's end.

KIRITI SENGUPTA

Orison

Vermilion marks her placing.
Blushing bride bows.

Elders exalt the esse of
her spouse–
sada suhagan raho!

Note: *Sada suhagan raho* (be blessed with your love/partner as long as you are alive) is a common way of blessing a newly married woman, usually by the elderly females of the Hindi/Urdu-speaking Indian families.

KIRITI SENGUPTA

The Y-Gene

My friends were aware of the wish I nurtured.
If I had a daughter,
I would name her *Srividya*!
I was not influenced by any actor.
Our prayer room hosted a dazzling
crystal *Sri Yantra* on the holy altar.

My wife's desires were girly too.
She wished to drape her daughter
in frilly dresses.
She had plans to find her girl
a groom in clover, so my wife could
live comfortably! Prior to her labor,
my mother-in-law keenly observed
my wife's navel, *Come on, it's a boy!*
It was a boy, a cute little one
of two and a half kilos.

To take care of the borderline weight,

special supplements were arranged.
My wife looked bright in pride.
We worshiped the *Narayana*
right after the holy bath.
My son is at school.
It's a co-education convent.
After school he tells his mother,
Girls sit on the left side.

KIRITI SENGUPTA

Womb

With every earthquake I realize
I fail to pay much attention to
my Mother.

She has a right to take me into her
again.

I know she will take
enough care
as she did before.

Oh, world! You may comment on material loss,
only Mother understands her rupture pain.

LAWRENCE SCHIMEL

Fairy Tales For Writers: The Little Mermaid

She gave up her voice for him,
learning to mimic the minimalist style
he advocated in his workshops.

They met at a conference.
He was one of the guest lecturers,
and all during his talk about passion
and craft, he kept his eyes on her.

In the one-on-one discussion of her work,
he complimented her form
and said she showed tremendous promise.
The things he could show her...
His deep-timbred voice was full of assurances
and innuendoes, and she succumbed to both.

She slaved to scrape together
enough money to join the MFA
where he taught, working double shifts

as a waitress that sent sharp pains
shooting up her legs from being on her feet
all day and night. She had no time to write.
But she bore it all silently, buoyed by the memory
of their time together at the conference,
and the promise the future held.

At the cocktail party, the night before
the first day of classes, where the students were
to meet and mingle with the faculty and each other,
he introduced her to his wife,
who had also once aspired to write, but now
was content to remain in his shadow,
to be seen by his side when he won awards and
to look the other way when he followed
his wandering eye.

MAAZ BIN BILAL

Muslimah
a poem in six voices

I
The Saudi in the Audi

Yeah, you're right, I drove that Audi,
in prison, I am, I am the woman of Saudi!

Yeah, read this right,
and hold on tight,
as I make some way,
for my sista's fight.[1]

II
The Hijab Examination

On the third of May,
in great dismay,
I went to attest
for the sake of protest,

to my own shame,
I sat the premed test.

To appear for an exam,
I had to undergo the sham
of having to reveal,
to forcibly peal,
my second skin,
in front of the non-kin.

A turbaned man,
also sat the exam.
His beard and headgear,
had not my scarf's smear.

III
The Researcher from Syria

I heard her in Newcastle,
at a conference
on practising
the PoCo way.

Her work, on
women's health
in Aleppo,
Syria.
The data she'd collected, so
painstakingly,
was from earlier times of peace.

Now, absolutely

meaningless.
Tending more to a cipher each day.

As she presented it,
devoid of referent,
she could not hold back her tears,
which flowed freely to express
her grief for the primeval.

Aleppo, now rubble, and desolate,
had, till recently, been
the world's oldest,
inhabited city.

It filled her voice, that dust, it choked her throat.

A medical anthropologist,
the numbers in her hands, they used to be women,
now meaningless.

The numbers in her hand, they used to be women,
people, who were no more.
They'd returned to that dirt from which they came.
Made of flesh, woman like man, man like child, all gone back to the earth, their mother.

IV
Mothers of Gaza

In Gaza there are no sons.
In Gaza we want daughters.
In Gaza let's not procreate.
In Gaza they've an expiry date.

V
Call to Mrs. Rehman

Hello, Mrs. Rehman!
What date is Eid this time?
We're all so missing the *biryani* from last year!
And the *kebabs*, just to die for!
And Mr S, here, just swears by your *shir*!
You know I tried your *qorma* recipe?
But it's just not the same!
I can't ever get it right!

VI
Right in the Face

Oh yes, I got it right in the face,
that bullet that sought to end an idea.
But all the love out there made me stronger,
all fears and 'my hopelessness died on that day.'[2]
I fly now, I educate, I teach girls, to blow the world away.

[1] The poem was written when it was still illegal for women to drive in Saudi Arabia.

[2] From the speech of Malala Yousafzai delivered at the UN youth assembly on 12 July 2013.

MADHU RAGHAVENDRA

Bride Wanted Ads

The Hindu Marriage Act has
no mention of the warm samosa
or the amount of ginger in tea.
This etiquette comes from our rich culture.
But all this is of no use if she cannot deliver a boy.
A girl will be an added cost.

Every square centimetre will cost extra
Colour will cost extra
Place will cost extra
Space will cost extra
Every word will cost extra
Sorry! Evry ltr wl cst xtra

Brid wntd fr BRAHMIN boy
Wrkg MNC, v.h'som
h'ly edu ab'd, stld ab'd
from afl. Biz fmly
Seek veg, vrgn cultrd b'ful tal fair
slim girl fr houswife, non fb user.

Kndly snd detals wth recnt phto
to thisiswhoweare@castenobar
butbrahminpreferred.com

MADHU RAGHAVENDRA

Conflict

Wars are no aphrodisiacs
then why do it. Maniacs!
Let us guillotine sex for peace.
Let the government and rebel forces
settle for a peaceful stride
before they get to hump and ride.
Let my tribe be protected by peace
not by arms.
I am a woman; I can freeze civil wars
between my thighs
let your arousal increase
peace.
Once we win over your gory arms
let's make love in peace.

Note: The concept of 'sex strike' is an age-old method of non-violent resistance, as evident in Aristophanes' classical Greek play Lysistrata, and most recently in the Spike Lee film Chi-Raq (2015). This poem was inspired by one such movement to bring back peace in South Sudan in 2014.

MADHU RAGHAVENDRA

Gālè
for Poge Karso

The wrap and weft of stories
knit life and lore tightly.
Automated looms loom,
the dust on our hands draws debt
and dullness takes over.
The assembly lines kill culture,
societies now come in the same clothes.

She meditates like a mountain.
One end of the loom tied to the window,
an antelope of light leaps looking for a companion;
the other end to her spine.
Her nerves run through the universe.
There are no permanent fixtures,
the voice of her fabric is untamed.

Her dyes don't bleed; she bleeds love
for daughters, brocades of rain,

fashion, decorative dashes, peacock plumes and
lakes of lilacs that drown man and his machines.
Her colours are infinite, her needles converse
in codes, migrate centuries
before she brings them home.

Her motifs are faceless revolutions.
No pamphlets are served, no slogans raised
yet her women blossom
at the dance of her tribe like wild orchids.
She owns no war, stitches boundaries and
harvests the sun on her loom,
yet none of her children weave a gālè.

Note: The gālè is the colourful wrap that is worn around the waist by the Galo women. The Galo are a central Eastern Himalayan tribe which primarily inhabit the West Siang, Lepa Rada, Lower Siang, East Siang, and Upper Subansiri districts of Arunachal Pradesh, in North East India.

MANIK SHARMA

Leaving

I often looked back
at the mountains we would leave,
and wonder if they'd still be there
when I come back.
I would hold Mummy's hands
when we would be in a flight—
her fears tethered to mine.

Thousands of blinking lights
we would see when the fear of
returning to their crowdedness,
slowly begin to take shape.
Such shapes are what fill
roaming pots of unnoticed
hate we grow up to be.

Ma, though more scared
than me, would open her eyes,
cup my chin in her hands, and smile

an unsure smile; but never, shiver.

I come and go alone now.
My fears are just mine, and
inside the shapes they have taken,
the windows to my mother's room
open and close. And in their throw
of air, unmixed with human breath

I shiver; even on the warm
mornings when I hastily dust printed
photographs of us together
to look at, and find in them
the mountains that have
now begun to depart.

MANIK SHARMA

Grandpa And Grandma Sit On The Veranda

Grandpa poached a rabbit once, before turning
vegan; that picture is still on the wall,

alongside the photo which confirms
he got Grandma as well.

Pictures don't speak in names, but memory
becomes an old man's commotion.

Grandma probably declined to having any of
her photos put up on the wall

or nobody asked her, I didn't.
I just wanted Grandpa and Grandma to sit

on the veranda, where loftiness of slow lives
could, perhaps, be discovered. Grandma's chemise

had leafy sketches, of crack-opened skies—

Grandpa, probably, struggled to tell the difference

and looked up, occasionally, as if to confirm
the cracks were not in his eyes.

If not for the rain, or the bread they had
for years broken together, they refused

to step back inside. It probably scared
them both, that their coffin-fitting clothes

seemed wrapped, rather than worn. It scared
Grandpa to think, how easy it would be, to not

miss her when she would be gone. It scared
him more than it would be easier for her.

They were angry at each other for getting old, and
for having crumpled skin that read like trashed paper.

Grandpa, though, still liked to tell us stories of how
he had grown through dark years, and that Grandma

at that time, was the woman closest
to the sun—her rabbits, wet, in his shade.

MILAN MONDAL

The Silent Lane

In every lane,
The fragrance remains unchanged.
Tonight she is ready to go with anyone
For bargaining is useless.

The insomniac little ones in her family
Yawn and smell the blossoms of devil's tree
Through the window with torn curtains.
The empty path brings no hope for her.

PARESH TIWARI

Cartography

At thirteen, she understands how rivers are born. Spends the night clutching a bedsheet between her legs. And when the fertile clay of her body breaks open, an ill-fitting bra is thrust her way. She spends weeks praying her breasts would go away.

A continent sprawling over a stretch of unbroken ocean, claimed by many, she knows she has to learn about borders and boundaries.

There's a peace treaty on the cut of her hair
follows the mountain ridge of shoulder blades
An armistice over the length of her skirt
covers the forest growing out of her ankles
A ceasefire over the neckline of her blouse
a school bag soldiers her bosom on bus rides

The shape of her claim changes with time. Days go by as she mourns the surrender of her voice. At sixteen, she learns to travel. Her fingers walk for miles over the unfamiliar trails of her own body. She spends the night strangling a strain of desire.

PARESH TIWARI

Surviving Marital Rape

Focus into the distance, where a fan whirrs away incessantly. A spider weaves around the moth. Paint scabs over a wound on the ceiling.

Cleave the smell of his sweat from your skin as he pins you down.

Turn your face away. There's dust gathering in hard to reach corners of the room. Look at the cracked spine of 'The Bell Jar'. Notice how the bookmark sticks out at an obtuse angle from the 142nd page.

Bite down your tongue while he unhooks your bra.

Dig your nails into the soft of your palms. Or tear holes into the stained bed sheets. Wipe away flecks of saliva from your face.

And when he pushes inside you?

Remember to Breathe. Wait. Breathe. Stop breathing.

Hear him grunt. Roll over. Clench the ache in your belly.

Gather your skin and your splintered bones. Stitch them into a sail-boat. Toss them into an aquarium for a goldfish to brush by. Watch a lull spill over its fins.

Or you could say, 'No'. Loud enough for the walls to come crashing down.

RAJA CHAKRABORTY

Of Houses

The old house blushed
Twilight hues painting a shy smile
Across its worn walls
Reminiscent of the first night
You had crossed the threshold
To call this your own

Crimson footsteps
Leaving indelible impression
On the floor
As they walked past the door
Into the inner sanctum
Of age-old acceptance

Bricks, myriad bricks
That's how houses grow and find soul
To become one with the flesh of
Sacrifice

RA SH

Andro And Estro

Androgen and Estrogen
met over a cup of Energen.
You know how macho
Androgen is.
And how feminine
Estrogen is.

Androgen complained.
These males are horrible.
A little extra of me and
they turn rapists.

Estrogen complained.
Same with the women.
A little extra of me and
they fall for Prince Charming.

A riot was on in the city.
A mob came.

Jealous of Androgen's huge phallus
they cut it off, leaving him to die
while watching them rape Estrogen.

Now, this city has vague males
and vague females inhabiting it.
And gender is a confusing concept.
Self fertilization is the in thing.

Emasculated Androgen and
stitched up Estrogen have fled.
They are said to be living
in an island named
Dopamine.

RA SH

Emasculated

In prison,
i am an anus,
lady with the pink blossom,
darling of the lawbreakers and the lawmen.
Amma amma mother of mine!
In this prison, your gallant son is but a hole.

In this manhole of human stench
where every cell sports a grave, in this vermin pit that knows
no lock, no key, no guard, no law, no messiah, no love,
i am but a shaft, orifice, cranny, chute
through which march the foot soldiers of manhood,
pillorying and ransacking in the name of
the god of male things, holding aloft
the flag that says
"Invasion, Incursion, Penetration!"

In prison,
my ass is a treasure

sought after by 1000 men.
Catcalls follow me, wolf whistles fly around me,
My ass is groped by 2000 hands and 20000 fingers,
probed, pressed, squeezed,
crushed, rubbed, pinched,
slapped, patted, exposed.

Creedless and classless, the ravaged male bum
is a vagina, veiled or bared, bruised or
painted, i am prime property, taken
against my will, branded by
the owner, emasculated,
feminized.

Amma amma mother of mine!
Pussy, they call my ass!
Lady, they call me!
Man or woman
am i?

RICCARDO DURANTI

A Battle Lost

She felt her mind curling up
        around the wind
and a kite was born out of her will
        freedom unraveled fast
        from her hands
        leaving a strong scent of disappointment
        under her nails…

RICCARDO DURANTI

Two-Ways Liberation

His world was a steep glass-pane
which she tried to climb over
disguised as a snail,
until – out of frustration –
she made up her mind
and knocked her shell
against his upright defense…

When she treads now
on the gleaming floor of his mind
a soft creaking
reminds her of a quickly-multiplying sharp ache;
how shattering the echo of her awareness
landing
on that cold jail-screen.

SANKET MHATRE

Bed No. 187

She was left like a half thought,
and because her name was a mumble of stuffed breath,
I called her 187.

She was a lonely prayer
searching for God at the entrance of hangar.
Her paper skin that kept melting into water
was enough to drown a generation of four-hundred beds.

An island whose language is a mishmash of silence,
she kept searching for her son, daughter-in-law and grandson—
now a safe distance away.

She was always hungry and gulped the half-cooked broth-like truth.
Regret tasted bitter but at least it tasted like home.

Later on, she chewed hunger for dessert, and smiled.

A night ago, she held my hand and cried—
If I die here, will you take me back to my village?
She handed me a letter with no address.

I have to leave, I said. *I'm cured.*
She smiled and wrapped her wrinkles around me
like that is the only gift she could give
before going to sleep.

SARABJEET GARCHA

The Girl Of Fifteen

for Jyoti Kumari

The heart her only guide, she spares
her body the desire to sprawl
under the neem tree back home.

The road her only prod, she dares
the tarmac vapours rising up
to become her noonday bandanna.

Her father on pillion, she flares
her way into the darkness the sun
pistons into her head.

The girl of fifteen cycles
her injured father home.

She cycles into the wrecking ball
of heat that an unseen operator
swings full throttle towards her.

She cycles over the mirages
that megapolises raise on every path
those like her would ever walk.

She cycles into the man-size
LCD screens that never
tire of flashing lies.

She cycles into the light
caught in the pages
of the Book of Miracles.

The girl of fifteen cycles
her dream of home, home.

She writes with her feet the names
of all the dead migrants into the DNA
of roads that stretch to eternity.

She writes the names of the lame
who've pawned themselves in a game
only the chess master understands.

She writes the one rule
only a woman knows by birth:
In my house, nobody dies of hunger.

She writes *thunder*
on the skin of the sky drummed
by the tears of the abandoned.

Pumping the pedals
as if to crush Death himself,
the girl of fifteen cycles
the souls of the wounded home.

SOUMIK KUMAR DE

An Ode To Skin

You that wrap the mind and soul
You that turn the world two
You that attract, you that cause to repel
You again that tempt, you that rent
You that shelter the babe
You too that is brutally raped.

> You smell, you reek.
> You spell, you seek.
> You toil, you sleek.
> You foil, you shriek.

You that smile, you that cry.
You that laugh, you that weep.
You that soothe the vibrant lust.
You that wait to be turned to dust.

You are admiration, you are passion.

You the effect, you the reason.

SOURADEEP ROY

For My Grandmother

You appeared suddenly: in the forehead of a classmate
smeared with sandal paste, your memory a sudden flash
in an old analog camera. Really, it's not me but my
forehead that misses you, misses the touch of your middle
left finger smeared with soil from the *tulsi* tree and some
Sanskrit chants of Krishna. Or was it Gopal? The exams
are going on well, *Dida*, but sometimes in the middle of
quoting Lukács, I wonder if your face has becomes more
lined—if the tributaries of lines have made little islands,
islands of islands. How are things back home? Have the
two of you finally made peace with each other —mother and you?

Taking sides was easier in childhood.
I hardly ever saw my mother. I was with you.

Let us weigh the scales now. Perhaps history will favour you
more for the same things the two of you did—working nine
to five, falling in love, and marrying out of caste
and out of class. If I have to take sides now, I have to weigh
history and a thousand -isms against relationships—

the objectively, objectively against the subjective. But really

Taking sides was easier in childhood.
I hardly ever saw my mother. I was with you.

In fact, it was difficult at ten to accept that you were not my mother.
Ever since you told me at eighteen that you too breast-fed me
since mother—well, I've repeated this far too many times,
exactly how I used to complain when I was young—
was hardly ever around, I have wondered if I'm
Oedipal towards you too. Keep this one request, will you?

Try and hang around while I am here. I need to see you dying.
Just as you saw me grow, I need to see you die.
After all, what is necessary is that I watch
you die, see death unfold on the bedside,
be the grandmother to you,
just as you were
a grandmother to me.

SUBHRASANKAR DAS

Zero

All the nets are not devised for all sorts of fish!

My aunt was an inefficient trap-maker.
Never did she learn the art of throwing nets,
but she could catch carp, salmon or climbing fish bare handed.
She would release the young ones
as if she could hear them scream.

She was trained to ignore
the scream of her youngest daughter,
and none came to rescue her
out of fear, shame and disgust.

My aunt could seamlessly figure out the difference
between the gutters of fish and snake.
She was trained to carry fear, shame and disgust.

In the evening, with a cup of tea,

my uncle would announce
how many points she gathered and for what.
Wearing a plastic smile,
she would faithfully preserve the certificates
and then watch him with her blank, inexpressive eyes.
Like a pit-viper, my aunt could suck the smell
of two different bodies concealed under his favourite perfume.

With a bottle of perfume,
she was last seen near the pond
on the day of *Dussehra*.

She was quiet and covered with mud.

Now, at night,
people hear my uncle shouting like a lunatic.
He leaves the house as if it's on fire.
He scrambles to the street
and beats his head repeatedly on the rugged milestone, saying,
Forgive me! Forgive me!
You got hundred out of hundred;

I am zero.

SUMALLYA MUKHOPADHYAY

Myths In The Family

Maa

A clock.
Her hour and minute hands stretch windows wide,
promise life to things she sees, believing
no one should suffer, no one should be made to suffer;
she plucks flowers that do not die, remaining
in folded memories of pages half-read,
as time stands still in the morning, smelling
basil, oregano, parsley, on steps her shadow takes.

Didi

A compass.
The North magnetic rests on the clockwork of her mother,
and in West she knits an oilskin, wearing
it on her way to South to discover empathy in wayward East;
but the directions aggregate in her, finding
a soul where the clock directs the afternoon tides,

sets the map of the world right, inspiring
many to compose songs in languages unheard.

Noor

An evening star.
If time maintains balance, the compass, its measure.
She paints her own canvas, blending
the fearless and selfless spirit of her mother and grandmother;
no older than they are, still quite young, granting
nights to townspeople in days of esurient sun.
She is the unheard songs and flowers undead, embodying
the generations of resilience in one complete self.

TIM KAHL

An Underdog In Training

As the big new hospital threatens to move in
and clear out the family businesses in its path,
I wonder if there is a code among predators.
Is stealth required or is it only necessary for
others to obey their desires? Coercion is such
a manly trait. Veblen saw it as an outgrowth
of the barbarian state—from warfare through
private property to control over other people's
bodies, mostly women, who stay at home and
get on with things. I have seen the great meals
...I have seen the sewn clothes...I have seen
the many lessons they took the time to teach.
Some say I have been a product of all this
business. It has left me here in this chair
stretching out my fantasies. I have to admit
I have no fantasy of capturing the grounds
of my neighbors. I have no hankering to make
them do as I please. I do not wish to erect
an oversized building in a distant land with

my foreign capital. I'm not budging. So when
I say, leave me to my knitting—does this make
me a feminist? Or am I someone who dislikes
seeing people be bothered and directed by
the aggressive? Tomorrow there may be
someone closing in, and I'm an underdog in
training who still believes in counter-punching.

UMAR NIZARUDEEN

On Tabassum, My Daughter Stumbling Upon The Word 'Consummation' In A Dictionary

Not for her
Ethereal glimpses
        Of roseate morning skies

Tridasan vihaya, the
        Crimson trails on the parting of her hair
Frolicsome
        dips in the pond

The pride of erect breasts
        Kissed by weary garlands of marigold

The insolence
        Of tender limbs

Not for her
The tender
        companionship of the blue god

Not for her

The all-consuming void
        Atop mount Kailasha

Whirlings of the Darvish, or
        Perversions of Foucault, Derrida

Not for her
Swan lake on
        Moonlit nights

Rose gardens of Shalimar,
        The love of Majnoon

Not for her
The Carrefours
        of Shahin Bagh and Taksim

Gazelle-eyed flights
        Across plastic borders

Not for her
The cosmic dance of
        Black hips

The flashing eyes and
        Slipping drapes

The luminous bazaars
        Of Scheherazade

Not for her
The jouissance
        of clickety fingers

The frolicsome Eid
        Of a thousand full moons

Not for her
The adolescent devotees
Of CR7

Or the Feigned anger
Of reunions

Not for her
Dreaming steeples
Of incunabula

The vermillion of freshly
Wiped tears

The pollen grains
of Behzad and Hafiz

Not for her
The mystic routes
of Baghdad

The miracle of
Jerusalem
The blue mosque
Or the red one
The pools of emerald
And jasper

Not for her
Stolen kisses
On the corniche
Simmering anger
Of the dark-eyed goddesses

For Her,
Consummatum est.

VIVEKANAND SELVARAJ

Bharat Mata

Bharat Mata was my classmate once. On independence days however,
I did not recognize her. Braces and the accompanying

smile, hanging off her sword like a traitor's gut,
Saree draped like white waves with

tri-color foam and a fiery ball on her usually
bare forehead, she would stand at the

assembly's centre, a statue outside
Time, the glitter of imitation

jewelry and kitschy crown,
demanding suspension

of our disbeliefs, that
it was the same Little

girl, who when snared

by the teacher's
roving eyes   and facing her extended cane

~~*Copy Cat Caught in act*~~
~~*Copy Cat Copy cat*~~
~~*Class Test Copy Cat*~~

~~*Rose Mary, right hand forward*~~

Wet herself in full view of the class
and did not turn up
the next three days.

ABOUT THE POETS

Abhay K. is the author of nine poetry collections, most recently of *The Alphabets of Latin America* (Bloomsbury), and the editor of *The Bloomsbury Book of Great Indian Love Poems, CAPITALS* and *New Brazilian Poems*. His poems have been published in several literary journals. His 'Earth Anthem' has been translated into over 50 languages. He has received SAARC Literary Award 2013 and was invited to record his poems at the Library of Congress, Washington DC in 2018.

Aditya Shankar was born and raised in India. His poetry, flash fiction and translations have appeared in journals and anthologies around the world. He has been nominated for Best of the Net and Pushcart Prize multiple times. His most recent book *XXL* (Dhauli Books, 2018) was shortlisted for the Yuva Puraskar (selected by Sahitya Akademi). Shankar's other books are *After Seeing* (2006) and *Party Poopers* (2014). His short films have participated in International Film Festivals. He lives in Bangalore.

Alan Britt has been nominated for the 2021 International Janus Pannonius Prize awarded by the Hungarian Centre of PEN International for excellence in poetry from any part of the world. Previous nominated recipients include Lawrence Ferlinghetti, Charles Bernstein and Yves Bonnefoy. Alan was interviewed at The Library of Congress for *The Poet and the Poem*. He has published 18 books of poetry and served as Art Agent for Andy Warhol Superstar, the late great Ultra Violet, while often reading poetry at her Chelsea, New York studio. A graduate of the Writing Seminars at Johns Hopkins University he currently teaches English/Creative Writing at Towson University. He can be reached at: alanbritt@comcast.net.

Allan Kolski Horwitz lives in Johannesburg. He writes in several genres and is an educator and activist as well. He is a member of the *Botsotso Publishing* editorial board and co-ordinator of the *Botsotso Ensemble's* performing arts programme. He has published four books of poetry – *Call from the Free State* (1979), *Saving Water* (2005), *There are Two Birds at My Window* (2012) and *The Colours of Our Flag* (2016); and written and directed several plays – *The Pump Room, Comrade Babble, Boykie and Girlie, Jerico, Book Marks and Taking Everything into Account.*

Alvin Pang, PhD is a poet, writer and editor whose broad creative practice spans over two decades of literary activity in Singapore and elsewhere. His writing has been translated into more than twenty languages. Featured in the *Oxford Companion to Modern Poetry in English* and the *Penguin Book of the Prose Poem*, his latest titles include *WHAT HAPPENED: Poems 1997-*

2017 and *UNINTERRUPTED TIME* (Recent Work Press: Australia, 2019). He completed his PhD in writing with RMIT University in 2020. His research interests include the possibilities of literary practice conducted across multiple languages, genres, careers and communities.

Amal Joseph Mathew hails from Kerala, India. His work has previously featured in Nether Quarterly and VAYAVYA. He is currently pursuing undergraduate studies in Bangalore.

Amit Shankar Saha is the author of three collections of poems titled *Balconies of Time* (Hawakal 2017), *Fugitive Words* (Hawakal 2019), and *Illicit Poems* (Pothi 2020). He has been nominated for the Pushcart Prize, the Griffin Poetry Prize, the Best of Net Anthology 2020 and his poems have been included in Best Indian Poetry Anthology 2018. He is the Editor-in-Chief of EKL Review and the Fiction Editor of Ethos Literary Journal. He has a PhD in English from Calcutta University and teaches in the English Department of Seacom Skills University.

Amlanjyoti Goswami's recent collection of poems *River Wedding* (Poetrywala) has been widely reviewed. His poetry has been published in journals and anthologies around the world. A Best of the Net nominee, his poems have also appeared on street walls in Christchurch, exhibitions in Johannesburg, an e-gallery in Brighton and buses in Philadelphia. He has read in various places, including New York, Delhi and Boston. He grew up in Guwahati, Assam and lives in Delhi.

Ammar Aziz is a poet and filmmaker from Lahore, Pakistan. His poetry has been published in *Poetry at San-*

gam, Wild Court, Muse India, Dhaka Tribune, among others, and has found space in several anthologies including *The Red River Book of Erotic Poetry, Shimmer Spring* and *Greening the Earth.* His poems have been translated into Russian, Tamil, Bangla, Spanish, Kannada and Urdu. His multi-award winning films have been screened in over a hundred countries at major film and art festivals.

Ankush Banerjee is a poet, serving Naval officer, and mental health professional, currently based at New Delhi. His maiden volume of poetry, *An Essence of Eternity* was published by Sahitya Akademi, New Delhi, 2016. His poems can be found in *Indian Literature, The Bombay Literary Magazine, Vayavya, Eclectica, Cha, Jaggery Lit, Dissonance Magazine* and elsewhere. He is currently working on a his second collection of poems, which attempts to explore and elucidate the problematic position of the Indian combatants during World War I and II.

Basab Mondal is a teacher by profession. He is from Kolkata. He is a bilingual poet and columnist who writes in English and Bangla. His poems, stories and translations have appeared in several anthologies and literary magazines. He writes to gratify his own inner self and the world around him serves as the cue.

Bibhu Padhi, a Pushcart nominee, has published sixteen books of poetry. His poems have appeared in magazines and anthologies throughout the English-speaking world, such as Contemporary Review, London Magazine, Poetry Wales, Stand, Wasafiri, America, The American Scholar, The Manhattan Review, Poet Lore, Poetry, Southwest Review, TriQuarterly, New Contrast,

Antigonish Review, Dalhousie Review, and Queen's Quarterly. He lives with his family in Bhubaneswar.

Boudhayan Mukherjee, a bilingual poet, author and translator, who started as literary secretary of Visva Bharati University, has published extensively in journals and newspapers since mid-seventies. His first book of verse, *Black Milk* (1990), was followed by five anthologies, a collection of short-stories and translations. He has represented Sahitya Akademi at various poetry readings and taught Creative Writing in English at IGNOU. He is the founding member and literary co-ordinator of Srijan, a literary platform in Kolkata. He has recently translated 157 visually impaired poets from Braille into English for an international anthology titled *Fountain of Light* to be brought out by Sparshanandan.

Chand is a poet and writer by passion and researcher by profession. They are interested in the intersection of development discourse and the lived experience of trans and queer folx. Occasionally, they daydream about a world without gender.

Chandramohan Sathyanathan (b.1986) is an Indian English language Dalit poet and literary critic based in Trivandrum, Kerala. His accolades include being on the shortlist for the Srinivas Rayaprol Poetry Prize 2016 and a fellowship at the International Writing Program (IWP-2018) at the University of Iowa. His book of poems titled *Letters to Namdeo Dhasal*, 2016, was on the shortlist for the Yuva Puraskar of Sahitya Akademi (Academy of Letters). He organizes literary meets of English poets of Kerala– both online and offline. In year 2016, OUTLOOK magazine profiled him as one of the high achievers from the Dalit community. *Love after Babel and Other Poems*, published in Canada in 2020, was awarded the Nicholas Gullien Outstanding Book Award by the Caribbean Philosophical Association (CPA).

Debarshi Mitra is a 25 year old poet from New Delhi, India. His debut book of poems *Eternal Migrant* was published in May 2016 by Writers Workshop and his second collection *Osmosis* was published in 2020 by Hawakal Publishers. His works have previously appeared or are forthcoming in anthologies like 'Kaafiyana', 'Wifi for Breakfast' , 'Best Indian Poetry 2018', 'Red River: Poetry of Dissent' and to poetry journals like 'The Scarlet Leaf Review', 'Thumbprint', 'The Punch Magazine', 'The Seattle Star', 'The Pangolin Review', 'Leaves of Ink', 'The Sunflower Collective', 'Coldnoon', 'Indiana Voice Journal', 'The Indian Cultural Forum' among various others. He was the recipient of The Wingword Poetry Prize 2017, The Srinivas Rayaprol Poetry Prize 2017 and was long listed twice for the TFA Prize.

Dibyajyoti Sarma is a poet, writer and translator based in Delhi. His translation of the five Assamese novellas of Indira Goswami is forthcoming from Niyogi Books.

Durga Prasad Panda is an accomplished bilingual poet, translator, critic whose works have appeared in the prestigious journals across the country and abroad. A significant voice of freshness, he is recognised among the foremost poets writing in Odia today who has attended several symposiums including World Congress of Poets in 2019. Most recently, he has edited a Reader for Sahitya Akademi on the lifetime's work of eminent poet Jayanta Mahapatra. His honours include Indian Literature Translation Award 2002 from Sahitya Akademi, Kalinga Literary Festival Award 2015, among others.

Dustin Pickering is founder of Transcendent Zero Press and founding editor of Harbinger Asylum. He is a former contributor to Huffington Post, a Pushcart and Best of the Net nominee, and recipient of honors from The Friends of Guido Gozzano. He is the author of several poetry collections including *Salt and Sorrow* (Chitrangi Publishers) and *Knows No End* (Hawakal Publishers). His fairy tale *The Red Velvet Robe* was published by Alien Buddha Press. He lives in Houston, Texas.

Goirick Brahmachari's debut collection of poems, *For the Love of Pork* (Les Editions du Zaporogue, Denmark) won the Muse India – Satish Verma Young Writer Award (Poetry) 2016. He is also the winner of the Srinivas Rayaprol Poetry Prize, 2016. Other collections of verses by Brahmachari include *joining the dots*, 2016, *Wet Radio and Other Poems*, 2017 and *A Broken Exit*, 2019. He is currently working on two collaborative volume of verses titled *The Nightwalkers* along with Debarshi Mitra and *Non Tribal / Tribal* with Avner Pariat. His poems and essays have appeared in various journals, magazines, blogs and pamphlets.

Gopal Lahiri is a Kolkata-based bilingual poet, critic, editor and translator with 22 books published mostly (14) in English and a few (8) in Bengali, including four jointly edited books. His poetry is also published across various anthologies as well as in journals of India and abroad. He has been invited in various poetry festivals. He is published in 12 countries and his poems are translated in 12 languages. He is the recipient of the Poet of the Year Award in Destiny Poets, UK, 2016, Setu Excellence Award, 2020, Pittsburgh, US and Indology Life-Time Achievement award, West Bengal, India.

Inam Hussain Begg Mullick is an award-winning poet, editor, composer, photographer, performance artiste and independent academician. He has authored *Roses for the Madhouse* (Cult of Beauty, 2010), *Winter's Electric Architecture* (Hawakal Publishers, 2016) and *The Magical Life of Inamorato* (Writers Workshop, forthcoming) and co-edited *Peacocks in a Dream: An Anthology of Contemporary Indian English Verse* (Erothanatos: The Alternative, 2020), *Freedom Raga 2020: 74 Poets pay Tribute to the 74th Edition of India's Independence* (Exceller Books, 2020) and *The Kolkata Cadence: Contemporary Kolkata Poets* (Hawakal Publishers, 2021).

K. Satchidanandan was a Professor of English in Kerala and later moved to Delhi to edit Indian Literature and later to be the Chief Executive Officer of the Sahitya Akademi . He was also Professor and Director, School of Translation Studies, IGNOU, Delhi and National Fellow at IIAS, Shimla. He has 34 collections of his poetry translated in 21 Indian and foreign languages. He has won 51 literary awards and Fellowships including Sahitya Akademi Award, Poetry for Peace InternationalAward from the Govt of UAE, Tata Litfest Poet Laureate Award and the Senior Fellowship from the Govt of India, besides Knighthood of the Order of Merit from the Government of Italy and India-Poland Friendship Medal from the Government of Poland. He is a Fellow of Kerala Sahitya Akademi. Website: www.ksatchidanandan.com.

Khal Torabully, author of 26 books, is an acclaimed pioneer of indenture studies. He has been exploring the field of inclusive indenture for some 30 years. He devised the first methodology articulating coolie and slave trades. He is an honorary patron of the Ameena Gafoor Institute of Indenture (UK).

Kinshuk Gupta, a medical student, uses the scalpel of his pen to write about his experiences as an undergraduate student. He is the Poetry Editor at *Jaggery Lit* and an Associate Editor at *Usawa Literary Review*. His work has been published or forthcoming in *The Hindu, Voice & Verse Poetry Magazine, Modern Haiku, Presence, Contemporary Haibun Online, Human/Kind*, among others.

Kiriti Sengupta is the editor-in-chief of the *Ethos Literary Journal* (*ELJ*). He is also a translator and publisher from Calcutta and Delhi. He has been awarded the 2018 *Rabindranath Tagore Literary Prize* for his contribution to literature. Sengupta has published eleven books of poetry and prose, two books of translation, and edited seven anthologies. For more, visit: kiritisengupta.com

Lawrence Schimel writes in both Spanish and English and has published over 120 books in many different genres–including fiction, poetry, non-fiction, and comics–and for both children and adults. His books have won the Lambda Literary Award (twice), the Crystal Kite Award from the Society of Children's Book Writers and Illustrators, and have been chosen for IBBY's Outstanding Books for Young People with Disabilities three times, among other honors. His writings have been translated into over thirty languages, including Icelandic, Maltese, Farsi, Kurdish, Basque, Macua, German, and Japanese. In addition to his own writing, he is also a literary translator.

Maaz Bin Bilal is a writer, translator, and academic. He is the author of a collection of poems, Ghazalnama: Poems from Delhi, Belfast, and Urdu (Yoda Press, 2019) and the translator of Fikr Taunsvi›s diary of his Partition days, Chhata Darya as The Sixth River (Speaking Tiger, 2019). His translation of Mirza Ghalib›s Persian long poem on Banaras, Chiragh-i-Dair is forthcoming (Penguin, 2021). Maaz teaches literary studies at Jindal Global University.

Madhu Raghavendra is a poet, curator and social activist based in India. He has authored three books of poetry, *Make Me Some Love To Eat*, *Stick No Bills*, and *Being Non-essential.* He is the founder of Poetry Couture, a poetry initiative that created free spaces for poetry in many cities of India, including the North East. He uses performance poetry as a tool to advocate human and environmental rights. He collaborates with global artists to create cross disciplinary poetry experiences. His poems have been set to classical music and contemporary dance. He conducts performance poetry workshops for young adults, and reads at many literary festivals across India. His works have been featured in many literary journals.

Manik Sharma was born and raised in the hills. He has been living a pretty flat life since writing for a living and to live.

Milan Mondal, from Bankura (West Bengal, India), is a young emerging littérateur and scholar. He is an Assistant Professor in the department of English at Narajole Raj College (Narajole, Paschim Medinipur, West Bengal, India). Besides being a professor, he has a passion for creative writing. His creative compass includes poetry, micro-story, essay etc. His poems have been included in various journals and magazines. He is one of the poets featured in *Shimmer Spring* (Ed. Kiriti Sengupta, Hawakal Publishers, 2020). He can be reached at: milanmindalapengnrc19@gmail.com.

Poet, artist and editor **Paresh Tiwari** has been widely published, especially in the sub-genre of Japanese poetry. A Pushcart Prize nominee, he has published two widely acclaimed collections of poetry. His collection of haibun *Raindrops Chasing Raindrops* is the recipient of the 'Touchstone Distinguished Book Awards – 2017'. He is the co-editor of the international haibun anthology, *Red River Book of Haibun, Vol 1*, and is the serving haibun editor of the online literary magazine *Narrow Road.*

Born and brought up in Kolkata, **Raja Chakraborty** is a bilingual poet. He holds a very senior position in Government service and still finds time to write, doodle, and play with words, punning being his forte. He has published four books of Bengali rhymes and two collections of English poetry, all of which have been well received and fetched critical acclaim.

Ra Sh has published three collections of poetry, *Architecture of Flesh* (Poetrywala), *The Bullet Train* (Hawakal) and *Kintsugi by Hadni* (RLFPA Editions). He co-translated Sri Lankan Tamil poems with Meena Kandasamy in a collection, *Waking is another Dream* and a collection of Malayalam Dalit stories, *Don't want Caste*

(Navayana). He has also edited a collection of Malayalam poems, *How to translate an earthworm* (Dhauli Books.) His collection of translated stories from Tamil, *Ichi Tree Monkey and other Stories* (Speaking Tiger), a play, *Blind Men Write* (Rubric Publications) and a chapbook "In the mirror, our graves" are in the pipeline.

Riccardo Duranti has long taught English Literature and Literary Translation at The University of Rome "La Sapienza." He is a well known translator from English and American Literature into Italian. Among his authors: Edward Bond, Elizabeth Bishop, John Berger, Raymond Carver, Caryl Churchill, Roald Dahl, Kae Tempest, Robert Coover and Richard Brautigan. He has also published five books of his own poems and haikus, and one of short stories. He writes both in English and in Italian. He lives in the Sabine hills and grows olives.

Sanket Mhatre has curated *Crossover Poems* – a multilingual poetry recitation sessions that unifies poets from different languages on a single platform. Apart from this, Sanket Mhatre has been invited to read at Kala Ghoda Arts Festival, Poets Translating Poets, Goa Arts & Literature Festival, Jaipur Literature Festival, Vagdevi Litfest, Glass House Poetry Festival, Akhil Bharatiya Marathi Sahitya Sammelan and many others. Besides curating & reciting, Sanket Mhatre has also created *Kavita Café* – a Youtube Channel that combines cinematic vision with visual poetry.

Sarabjeet Garcha is a widely published bilingual poet and the author of four books of poems, including *A Clock in the Far Past*, besides a volume each of translated poetry and translated prose. He has translated several American poets into Hindi, including W.S. Merwin and John Haines, and several Indian poets into English, among them Mangalesh Dabral and Leeladhar Jagoori. He has also translated more than fifteen Marathi poets into both Hindi and English. He was on the Panel of Critical Readers for the third edition of *Garner's Modern American Usage* (Oxford University Press, 2009). His work, including poems, translations, and essays, has appeared in *Versopolis, Modern Poetry in Translation, Words Without Borders, Asymptote, the Indian Quarterly, Domus India, the Centre for Stories' Journal, the Wire,* and *Scroll*, among others. Sarabjeet received a two-year fellowship in literature from the Ministry of Culture, Government of India. He is the founder and editorial director of Copper Coin, a multilingual publishing company.

Soumik Kumar De, a teacher by profession and poet by passion, writes poetry both in Bengali and English. So far his poems have been anthologized in national and international publications and web journals like *Setu, The Indian Review, Borderless Journal, Aulos:An Anthology of Poems, Caravan,* and *Insal* to mention a few.

Souradeep Roy is from Calcutta. He is currently pursuing his doctoral studies in London.

Subhrasankar Das (D.O.B.: 1st May 1986), an author, translator and teacher is a figure of distinct repute in contemporary literature. He authored three books of Bengali poems (*Tontukit, Baul molecules, Sfotikchhapa Phosphorus*) and translated remarkable literary pieces (*Bukhari, Monster of the jungle, Jamichhalang*).

His poems have been published in many literary and commercial mags and books of Kolkata, Tripura, Bangladesh, Assam and in various International journals. He is the awardee of Binay Padak, Banani Shahitto Somman, Tobu Ovimaan Sommanona. He is the editor of *Shadowkraft* (the first Bilingual literary webzine from NorthEast) and *Water* (the first International and multilingual Video-magazine from NorthEast, India).

Sumallya Mukhopadhyay is a doctoral candidate at the Indian Institute of Technology, Delhi. He celebrates spirit over being, silence over company, resilience over power. His poems have been published in *Aainanagar, Cafe Dissensus, The Neesah Magazine, The Bangalore Review, The Firstwriter Magazine, Muse India, Hibiscus: Poems that Heal & Empower, The Bombay Review* and few other places.

Tim Kahl is the author of *Possessing Yourself* (CW Books, 2009), *The Century of Travel* (CW Books, 2012), *The String of Islands* (Dink, 2015) and *Omnishambles* (Bald Trickster, 2019). His work has been published in *Prairie Schooner, Drunken Boat, Mad Hatters' Review, Indiana Review, Metazen, Ninth Letter, Sein und Werden, Notre Dame Review, The Really System, Konundrum Engine Literary Magazine, The Journal, The Volta, Parthenon West Review, Caliban* and many other journals in the U.S. He is also editor of Clade Song [http://www.cladesong.com]. He is the vice president and events coordinator of The Sacramento Poetry Center. He also has a public installation in Sacramento {In Scarcity We Bare The Teeth}. He plays flutes, guitars, ukuleles, charangos and cavaquinhos. He currently teaches at California State University, Sacramento, where he sings lieder while walking on campus between classes.

Umar Nizarudeen is with the University of Calicut, India. He has a Ph.D. in Bhakti Studies from the Centre for English Studies in JNU, New Delhi. His poems and articles have been published in *Vayavya, Muse India, Culture Cafe Journal of the British Library, The Hindu, The New Indian Express, The Bombay Review, The Madras Courier, FemAsia, Sabrang India, Ibex Press Year's Best Selection*, and also broadcast by the All India Radio.

Vivekanand Selvaraj recently moved to Beijing and would very much like to introduce himself as a poet but he constantly attempts to write fiction too. He writes in both English and Tamil and translates from Chinese and English to Tamil and also from Tamil to English. His work has appeared in *TBLM, Nether Quarterly* (Revival issue), *Bengaluru Review, Sonic Boom, Vayavya* and *The Freedom Review*. His debut collection of Tamil poems, *Sudhandhiram Oru Dabba* was released in January 2021 (Manalveedu Publishers).

NOTES

"The Pleasure Givers" and "A Maid's Monologue" by Abhay K. were first published in *Muse India* and his "Mysterious Lady of Konark" appeared in *Margutte* Italy.

"Blue" and "Myth of the Baker's Daughter" by Alan Britt were first published in *Wasafiri* (UK) and *Vermilion* (The Bitter Oleander Press, 2006) respectively.

"The Outsider" and "Trafficked" by Amit Shankar Saha were first published in *Fugitive Words* (Hawakal Publishers, 2019).

"Foetus" by Basab Mondal was first published in *Shimmer Spring* (Hawakal Publishers, 2020).

Bibhu Padhi's "All Through the Long Night" was published in his first book of poetry, *Going To The Temple* (1988).

Chandramohan Sathyanathan's poems "Plus-Sized Poem" and "Portrait of a Poet as a Young Woman" were first published in his collection, *Letters to Namdeo Dhasal* (Desire-paths, 2016).

"In Which We Eat," "In Which Ganga Explains" and "In Which Shikhandi Regrets His Decision" by Dibyajyoti Sarma are from his third poetry collection, *Book of Prayers for the Nonbeliever* (Red River, 2018)

"Her Body" by Durga Prasad Panda was first published in *Parallel Speech: Fifteen Younger Contemporary Oriya Poets*, ed.: Bibhu Padhi and Minakshi Padhi (Authorspress, 2014).

An earlier version of Goirick Brahmachari's "As I Watch the Road" was first published in *Gossamer: an anthology of contemporary world poetry* by Kindle Magazine.

"Fear of Lizards" by Inam Hussain Begg Mullick first appeared in *The Statesman.*

K. Satchidanandan's poems, "Burnt Poems" and "She inside Me" were first published in *The Missing Rib, Collected Poems, 1973-2015* (Poetrywala, Bombay, 2016). His poem "Non-negotiable" was first published in *Not Only the Oceans, New Poems 2015-18* (Do, 2018).

Khal Torabully's poems are excerpts from his *Voices from the Aapravasi Ghat: indentured imaginaries* (Aapravasi Ghat Trust Fund, 2013).

"Y-Gene" and "Womb" by Kiriti Sengupta first appeared in *The Common* (Oct, 2019) and *Du-kool* (ed. Marc Paltrineri, June-July 2015) respectively.

"Fairy Tales for Writers: The Little Mermaid" by Lawrence Schimel was first published in Schimel's chapbook, *Fairy Tales for Writers* (New York: A Midsummer Night's Press, 2007).

"Muslimah" by Maaz Bin Bilal was first published in *Muse India.*

Madhu Raghavendra's "Bride Wanted Ads" was first published in his poetry collection, *Make Me Some Love to Eat* (Red River, 2016). His poem, "Gālè," first appeared in *Joao Roque Literary Journal.*

Manik Sharma's poems, "Leaving" and "Grandpa and Grandma Sit On The Veranda," were first published in *The Land Below Water* (RLFPA Editions, 2017).

"The Silent Lane" by Milan Mondal was first published in Setu (Voices Within, 2021).

Ra Sh's poems, "Andro and Estro" and "Emasculated," were first published in *Kintsugi by Hadni* (RLFPA Editions) and

A Strange Place Other Than Earlobes: an anthology of English poems by five Malayali poets (Sampark, Kolkata, 2015) respectively.

"The Girl of Fifteen" by Sarabjeet Garcha was first published in *Singing in the Dark*, edited by K. Satchidanandan and Nishi Chawla (Vintage, 2020).

"On Tabassum, my Daughter Stumbling upon the Word 'Consummation' in a Dictionary" by Umar Nizarudeen was first published in *FemAsia*.

Shamayita Sen is a Delhi based poet, lecturer, and PhD research candidate (Department of English, University of Delhi). She writes about grief and mourning, longing for her father's lap. Most of her poems that are now a part of her début collection, *For the Hope of Spring* (Hawakal Publishers, 2020) were written with a kind of guilt and restlessness as India suffered through the pandemic induced lockdown and Amphun last year. The government's apathy affects her more than her writing can contain. Her creative pieces on gender violence and mental health are inspired by traumatic experiences of her acquaintances and herself. Her research articles and poems have appeared in various avenues in India and abroad. She can be reached at shamayita.sen@gmail.com.